W9-ATX-052

Recovering from Depression

Recovering from Depression

Forty-Nine Helps

ROBERT W. GRIGGS

RESOURCE *Publications* · Eugene, Oregon

RECOVERING FROM DEPRESSION
Forty-Nine Helps

Copyright © 2019 Robert W. Griggs. All rights reserved. Except for brief quotations in critical publications or reviews, no part of this book may be reproduced in any manner without prior written permission from the publisher. Write: Permissions, Wipf and Stock Publishers, 199 W. 8th Ave., Suite 3, Eugene, OR 97401.

Unless otherwise noted, biblical quotations come from the King James Version of the Bible. References marked NRSV are taken from New Revised Standard Version Bible, copyright © 1989, Division of Christian Education of the National Council of the Churches of Christ in the United States of America. Used by permission. All rights reserved worldwide.

Resource Publications
An Imprint of Wipf and Stock Publishers
199 W. 8th Ave., Suite 3
Eugene, OR 97401

www.wipfandstock.com

PAPERBACK ISBN: 978-1-5326-8346-6
HARDCOVER ISBN: 978-1-5326-8347-3
EBOOK ISBN: 978-1-5326-8348-0

Manufactured in the U.S.A.   04/18/19

For My Brother

Walter S. Griggs, Jr.

Teacher, Writer, and Mentor

Contents

Introduction

DEPRESSION DESTROYS JOY AND brings pain. I know this from my own life. I also know that depression's progress is not inevitable. Depression can be halted and turned back, much that was lost can be recovered, and new happiness can be found in life. Life can be even better than it was before. My story tells how this has happened for me, what has helped me, and—especially—how others have helped me.

When I started to write this book, my goal was to have fifty short pieces, brief essays about different aspects of my recovery. I knew that some pieces—like my account of banging my head against the wall of the ER during my first hospitalization—would reflect the pain of my illness and be hard to write. Others—like the story of a sermon where my intended word *trucking* came out as an expletive that rhymed with it—would be lighter and fun to tell.

As the book progressed, fifty of what I came to call "Helps" seemed more and more like a reasonable goal. Fifty would be an accomplishment, like reaching one's fiftieth birthday or visiting all fifty states. But as I drew closer to fifty, I realized that my recovery would benefit if I stopped at forty-nine.

Stopping one short of my original goal defies my depression. As a child, I learned self-esteem based on achievement, which meant that I had to reach each goal and then set the next goal higher. As an adult, I continued to escalate demands on myself until I had a mental health crisis and needed to be hospitalized. There were other causes, physical as well as mental, but this need to achieve showed no mercy. Stopping with Forty-Nine Helps would show I've freed myself from these demands and have become comfortable with who I am.

Unfortunately, the reality of my recovery is more complicated. The truth is that I've made progress in letting go of unrealistic goals and escalating demands, but I'm still not totally free of them. The same is true about my recovery from depression in general. In my life before I was hospitalized, I would have made recovery a goal, like crossing the finish line of a race. "Look, everybody, I've recovered from depression. I came in first. Come and see my gold medal." But I'm not going to get a gold medal, and I'm learning to be OK with not standing on the winner's platform.

I've learned that for me recovery from mental illness is not a finish line: it's a way of life. I've made substantial progress. I claim this for myself because it's true and real. Yet some days my depression reasserts itself, not like the hell it once was, but it's there. On balance, my life is so much happier and fuller than it once was, maybe than it ever was. I can savor so many good things in my recovery, while accepting that I'm in it for the duration.

It's a journey that started fourteen years ago with my first hospitalization for major depression and generalized anxiety disorder. After a terrible time in the ER, I was admitted to a locked psych unit. That night I had the first real sleep I'd had in months. With the medications I'd been given, I didn't so much fall asleep as get knocked unconscious. Nevertheless, the night was so much better than all the nights of lying awake, clenched and cringing, reviewing an unending loop of all the ways I'd embarrassed myself, let other people down, and behaved shamefully. After I woke up, it took me a while to get oriented, to find my clothes, and to start getting dressed. I looked around for my belt, and then I remembered it had been taken from me. I'd forgotten for a moment where I was.

After breakfast, I met some of the other patients and fell into conversation. Along with many random things, we talked about ourselves and our illnesses. Later, in the more structured setting of group therapy, I found myself opening up about how much I was hurting and how much I feared the future. Such openness was new behavior for me, contrary to the denial and secrecy that I had learned as a child. Learning how to take openness out into my everyday life, to share how I feel with people I trust, has been an essential part of my recovery.

After my discharge from the hospital, I participated in a two-week day program, where I lived at home and went to the hospital each weekday for group therapy and various mental health education programs. The psychiatrist I was assigned to encouraged me to go back to the church where I was the minister as soon as I left the day program, maybe start back part-time for a few weeks, maybe get some more help, but go back.

I ignored what he said about going back part-time and tried to pick up where I left off. Though most people were trying hard to be kind, I felt like jagged words were being scraped across my skin at every meeting. After a week, I could not continue and I was on the verge of a relapse. With great generosity and in gratitude for the twenty-five years I had served as their pastor, the church leadership gave me three months off, full pay and benefits, in the hope that with enough time to rest and recover I could come back. Toward the end of the third month, I had a phone conversation with our church moderator. I told her that I felt great and was eager to return to work.

As soon as I put the phone down, I knew that I'd made a mistake. My symptoms exploded, and I was readmitted to the psych unit within a couple of days. This failed experience of trying to return to work—too much, too soon—has served as a basic lesson for me in managing my depression. I have learned to attend to stress triggers, and I recognize that saying no can be an affirmation of self-worth. My second hospitalization was my last, and I believe how I have learned to practice depression management is a major reason why.

I've kept each of my Forty-Nine Helps short because of my experience early in recovery. At that time, I found it hard to focus or stay with any task for very long. The self-punitive thoughts racing in my brain kept drawing my attention inward, away from the world outside. To stay focused, I looked for small tasks, like the daily reading of a few scriptures from the Bible. These short readings gave me a sense of accomplishment, made me feel better about myself and more in control of my life. If you are in a similar place, I hope what I've written can do the same for you. Though the topics and chronology of Forty-Nine Helps are in a loose order, they are mostly independent of each other. If you see a topic that may help you right now, I encourage you to read what I have to say about it regardless of where it comes in the book.

A little more about who I am will help you understand my choice of topics. I am an ordained minister in the United Church of Christ, and I live with my spouse, a retired RN. We have two married adult sons, who have both been a source of ongoing support for me in recovery. Given the role that genetics plays in mental illness, we have been open with them about mental illness, both my own and that of other members of our family.

We are fortunate to live in the Twin Cities of Minneapolis and St. Paul. This isn't because of the weather—though bright sun sparkling on fresh snow can do a lot of good for your mood provided you have a really heavy coat—but because it's the home of Vail Place, which offers many services for people seeking psychiatric recovery. Vail Place's two clubhouses, based on the model of Clubhouse International, provide places where people living with mental illness are accepted as a valued part of the community. As you read this book, you will learn more about Vail Place and why it is so important to me.

A few years ago, I wrote *A Pelican of the Wilderness: Depression, Psalms, Ministry, and Movies.* The book describes my time on the psych unit and the early days of my recovery. It focuses on my recovery of faith, how the psalms have been essential to that recovery, and how I was able to return to serving a church after a year and a half of working on my recovery.

The book you are holding has a wider focus. I hope its lessons on recovery will help both those living with depression and also those who share their lives with us. I know that many who will pick up this book have a faith tradition different from my own or have no faith tradition at all. I try to be respectful to all and open to all. We are united by the damage that depression has done to our lives.

I can't get back the pleasure and the time depression has stolen from my life, and I continue to live with depression. This is part of the truth of my life. It is also true that my life is fuller, certainly more honest and open, than it has ever been. Most days, it is also happier. I hope that in sharing what I've learned I can help others living with depression find the same joy and fullness in life.

Like recovery, this book would not have happened without the help of many people. My wife, Susan, read multiple drafts and corrected a multitude of errors. My sons, Tom and David, gave me their support and encouragement, as well as practical suggestions about how to make the book better. Chad Bolstrom, Uptown Clubhouse Director at Vail Place, and Stefano LoVerso, Development Director at Vail Place, helped make sure I described my beloved clubhouse accurately. Gordeen Gorder, my editor, not only prepared my manuscript for publication but also made many suggestions that clarified and strengthened it. Matt Wimer, Assistant Managing Editor at Wipf and Stock Publishing, was always quick to answer my questions and invaluable in moving this project to publication. I thank them all. I also thank the members of Vail Place Uptown who have taught me so much about recovery. I am deeply grateful.

Help 1

Defining Yourself

I DO NOT LET my depression define me. I am so much more than a mental illness. If we were on a playground and my depression got on one end of the seesaw and I got on the other, my end would drop quickly to the ground and my puny depression would shoot up into the air like a little rocket. It's fun to imagine depression soaring skyward, starting to sputter, flipping over, accelerating nose downward, and being knocked into smithereens by a crash landing! There's so much more to me than my illness.

That wasn't always so. There have been moments when my depression was all-consuming. When I waited in the hospital ER about to be admitted to the psych unit, depression raged in my mind. The pain was unbearable. To relieve it, I started banging my head against the concrete wall of my cubicle, just as earlier in the day I'd been banging my head against the tile wall of the shower at home. At that time, the depression and I were one.

But we soon separated. Oh yes, the depression was still very much with me, but we were no longer one. I knew this on my first morning in the hospital when I woke up after a nurse stuck her head in my room and asked perkily, "Are we feeling suicidal?" What a question to wake up to! And the "we"—was she planning on joining me if by chance I did feel suicidal? Was I special, or did she just go down the hall asking each patient in turn if we were feeling suicidal? Was she starting a club? It was all too much and too weird not to laugh. If I could laugh that way, put a little daylight between myself and my weird new world, then depression no longer owned all of me.

Later that morning, I had my first hospital breakfast. Of course, with no belt or shoelaces, I looked a little shabby, but then again several other customers dining at adjoining tables were wearing pajamas, robes, and hospital slippers with traction treads on the bottom. What kind of restaurant was this? It was all so strange. Whatever I was feeling then, it wasn't my depression. It was more like what it would feel like to be walking down the yellow brick road with Dorothy in the wonderful Land of Oz.

These memories remind me how quickly my depression stopped defining me. Before the morning was over, I was hanging out with people, maybe not using top-drawer social skills but, nonetheless, being social. Depression had failed to crush me and demolish who I was. I was so much more than an illness, just too big for it. Yes, it knocked me down and knocked me down again, but I got back up each time, and here I am, moving along in recovery.

I need to find words to talk about my depression that limit its power over me. There is a fraught history between words and mental illness. We know how words and phrases have been used to taunt and belittle us: mad, nuts, freak, crazy, loony, bonkers, spastic, psycho, crackers, deranged, demented, a head case, a whack job, off your rocker, not all there, out to lunch, weak in the head, has a screw loose, nutty as a fruit cake. The list of insults goes on and on. Mental illness is a particularly fertile field for those who want to use words to hurt.

There are better words, words that aren't cruel, words that don't magnify the power of mental illness. For example, the National Alliance on Mental Illness (NAMI) booklet *Hope for Recovery* suggests saying "people living with mental illnesses" instead of "mentally ill" and "person living with schizophrenia" instead of "schizophrenic."[1]

Following this guide, I say that I'm "a person living with depression." The language NAMI offers separates me from depression and mental illness in a way that's true to my experience, making it clear that my depression does not define me.

When I say that I'm living with depression, I'm also saying that my life is more than this disease. It feels much the same as saying I'm living with borderline high blood sugar. I can do things to control the blood sugar, and I am. In living with depression, I can do things to control depression, and I am. Neither disease comes close to dominating my life or defining who I am. I was brought up not to brag, but the truth is so many things are more interesting about me than the fact that I am living with depression.

I've met people in recovery from mental illness who are writers, musicians, painters, photographers, sculptors, weavers, potters—artists of all kinds. When you ask them what's up, they'll start telling you about their art or an upcoming show. They don't tell you about their illness. Likewise, I've met people in recovery who are returning to their jobs or professions and people who are developing all manner of new skills in preparation for reentering the workforce or getting better jobs. If you ask them what's up, they'll tell you about a new computer class or a job interview, not about their mental illness.

Yes, if the conversation continues and you take time to get to know these people in recovery, they're likely to say something about the mental illness they're living with, maybe that at times it's still very hard. They might tell you that what they learned living with mental illness has inspired and sustained them in their art and their work. Many of these people would tell you who has helped them in recovery and how grateful they are for that help. Whatever they say, they make it clear that their lives are not being defined by the mental illness they live with. We are so much more than that.

HELP 2

Being Authentic

ONE NIGHT, AS I was sitting by myself at a table on the psych unit eating a free ice-cream bar, a social worker came and sat down across the table from me. She was about my age and seemed quite comfortable sitting there, taking a break during her shift. Maybe I should have offered her a bite of my ice-cream bar, but I was pretty foggy headed, and the details of good manners were beyond me.

She started talking. At first I couldn't follow what she was saying. When I finally got up to speed, I heard her telling me that I was doing well in the hospital. That was news to me. She said that she had been watching me (which felt a little spooky) and that she was glad that I had made friends on the unit. Well, I guess I had, but I was tired and just not up for talking. My mind drifted away for a time. I remember thinking seriously about getting another ice-cream bar for myself.

Then something she said caught my attention. She was talking about authenticity and about how hard it is to be someone other than yourself. When she said this, I knew that she was on to me. She could see I was a fake, pretending to be a conscientious, loving pastor, when in reality I had just been doing the bare minimum to get by and get paid. I feared she was going to tear into me. Well, let her. No way was she going to be as good at doing that as I was already. I had lain awake night after night loathing myself as a liar, a cheat, and a phony. I'm not sure that I had any new pain left to give her.

The social worker didn't want any of my pain. She told me that I deserved a break and some good rest and that it was exhausting to try to be someone other than who you are. Of course, this could have been an accusation, more proof that she was on to me, but she didn't say it that way. It felt more like she was talking about something that was true of everyone, herself included. By the time the conversation was over—I never did get that second ice-cream bar—I felt better about myself.

Being authentic, like being thin, is easier said than done. Raised to meet the expectations of my father by achieving success after success, I didn't have a lot of practice in learning what I really wanted to be or do. From gaining my dad's approval, I graduated to trying to please people in general, trying to be what everybody wanted me to be. It's hard to do that when different people make different, sometimes conflicting, demands on you. The social worker was right: being someone other than yourself is exhausting.

In *I Thought It Was Just Me (But It Isn't)*, Dr. Brené Brown describes exactly what this was like for me:

> We are often so influenced by what other people think and so overwhelmed with trying to be who other people need us to be, that we actually lose touch with our sense of self. We lose our grounding. We lose our authenticity.[2]

In recovery I've been trying to find my way to authenticity. The dietary department at the hospital gave me unwitting help in doing this. The first morning of my first hospitalization, I awoke fuzzy headed and disoriented by whatever drug they'd used to zonk me to sleep. I stumbled around, managed to get dressed, and made it out to the lounge in time for breakfast. Somebody showed me where the trays were, and I found the one with my name on it. I guess this made me a regular. I took off the plastic cover and found French toast and three strips of bacon.

I love bacon, but like cigarettes, we don't have bacon at our house. I ate the first two slices quickly, and then I took my time enjoying the third. Sheer pleasure! I'll believe that my recovery started at that moment. Pleasure had broken in on me, the absolute real thing. When I say that I like bacon, you can smell the authenticity.

Bacon today, maybe there'll be bacon tomorrow; you'll need to get out of bed and go see. I'm really looking forward to the next time we have bacon! I'm a passionate believer that having something to look forward to, something that truly gives you pleasure, is a key element in recovery. This was brought home to me with simple eloquence by an elderly woman I met during my first hospitalization. She had a Styrofoam bowl full of mixed nuts that she shared with me. She told me that the glass bottle they had come in was deemed by the staff to be dangerous, so they doled the nuts out to her one Styrofoam bowl at a time. Toward the end of our conversation, she told me about a mistake she had made, "I took pleasure for granted. That was my big mistake. Take your eye off pleasure, and you will lose it." This insight into the nature of pleasure has done much to sustain my recovery.

At Vail Place, the clubhouse for people living with mental illness that I will describe more fully in Help 15, we are careful not to take our eyes off pleasure. For example, we have social recreation where members can sign up to go to a play, a movie, restaurant, a Twins game, or go dancing or camping—the list is almost endless. Depending on what you like, what gives you pleasure, there's a good chance that some activity will be on the list that you can sign up for and start looking forward to.

There is a caveat to having something to look forward to: the pleasure has to be authentic. I might impress people if I said I was looking forward to eating truffles in cream, but it's really bacon that gets me up in the morning. I'm learning to love classical music, but when I'm finished writing this chapter, I'm going to enjoy watching our Minnesota Twins on TV—at least until the game is hopeless. On a more professional level, I don't mind going to a preaching workshop, learning how to emit less hot air and more wisdom is always a good thing, but what I really look forward to is hanging out at lunch with some old friends.

I find tremendous authenticity in saying these things. Moreover, honesty about pleasure leads to honesty about other more complicated things. These days I can enjoy a day's work even when there are disappointments and frustrations. As long as I can honestly say there's something worthwhile that I'm trying to accomplish in my work, I can take pleasure from doing it.

In trying to be more authentic, examples of truly authentic people are a great help to me. I remember one of my elderly parishioners who told me that the doctor had asked her what she might be able to do to gain some weight. "Drink more brandy Alexanders," was her totally authentic answer. Another time the doctor told her that she should watch her cholesterol. "Doctor, I'm a hundred years old. Don't you think that I'm past the point that I need to worry about cholesterol?" Over the years, life had scraped away every bit of phoniness and pretense from this remarkable woman. I want to be like her.

On the other end of the age spectrum, there are small children who have taught me about authenticity, maybe because they haven't had time yet to accrue any phoniness. I remember a first grader at a Christmas pageant rehearsal telling his parents firmly and clearly, "I don't want to be a cute little lamb. I was a cute little lamb last year. I want to be a shepherd." You go, kid! There is something so deeply authentic about knowing and saying what you don't want and what you do want.

I want bacon, and I don't want to be a cute little lamb. I can't be more authentic than that.

HELP 3

Learning to Trust

MY RECOVERY RHYTHM IS to balance emotional work with pleasure and relaxation. Telling stories does this for me. I have a favorite story that will be a good break after the first two Helps, and it will serve as an introduction to this one.

A few years ago, I had cataract surgery. The pamphlet I was given about the surgery included helpful eye diagrams and a timetable for using eye drops. There was also a jolting declaration: "Whatever it feels like, your eyeball is not being removed."

Until I read this pamphlet, it had not crossed my mind that my eyeball was in danger of being removed during surgery. After all, I was having the surgery done by a highly recommended surgeon in a clinic, not in the kitchen by a friend who'd just thumbed through *Cataract Surgery for Dummies*. Now I worried about whether I had been told the truth about my eyeball's permanence. Could I trust the surgeon? Was the reassurance in the pamphlet a trick? I imagined the operating room being like my dentist's office, with several patients being worked on at once. Eyeballs were being popped out all over the place. How did I even know that I'd get my own eyeball back? And if they mixed the eyeballs up, would I at least get one that matched my good eye?

So many worries. But then it occurred to me what the pamphlet's authors were trying to do. Their reassurance showed that they'd been to this cataract-removal rodeo before. They knew some patients were afraid that eyeballs were being popped out during surgery, and they were trying to head off this fear. Understood this way, their promise that my eyeball was going to stay put was professional and confidence inspiring. Their foresight was a reason to trust them.

Well, I had the surgery and found to my delight that the pamphlet was not lying: my eyeball was still right there where I had left it. In fact, not only was my eyeball still there, but it was working better. The bright colors that had faded away were sharp and clear again. The pamphlet had not lied, and I had been wise to trust the surgeon.

That's my story. I wish I could say that it has been as easy for me to resolve my trust issues around depression. Sadly, that's not the case. Mental illness is toxic to trust; it isolates you and leaves you feeling unworthy of help. How could I be open when I was so ashamed of what I had to say? What possible confidence did I have that others would forgive me or even understand me? I simply couldn't trust myself to tell my family how badly I was hurting. I didn't know the words, I didn't want to hurt them, and I didn't have the energy.

Finally, just before I was hospitalized, the pain in my head became so great that in panic and urgent desperation I did try to reach across to my wife. But it was too late. In my panic I couldn't put the right words together. She tried to understand and tried to reach for me. She wanted to grab hold and keep me from falling, but I had already slipped away.

I landed in the hospital and woke up to the rubble of my life. Wherever I turned in that strange place, I found a locked door. There was no escaping other people. Whether it was the meds, the impact of all that had happened, the feeling that I had nothing left to lose—I don't know. But I do know that I opened up. When other patients told me their stories, I told them mine. I was honest without thinking about it.

Later in group therapy there was a kind of truth momentum. After others tell the hard truth about how they've been living, you can't make stuff up about yourself. At least I couldn't. I remember a mom with postpartum depression. She was crying as she told us she was too scared to hold her baby. I remember a young woman carefully rolling up a sleeve to show where she'd cut herself. I remember a sharply dressed man crying as he told us how hard it is for him to be a salesman without the jolt of energy that meth had given him. With each of their disclosures, I trusted their truth, and I was moved to respond with my own.

In recovery, I have tried to take what I learned about trust on the psych unit into my life beyond the locked doors of the hospital, where there is always the risk that one will trust the wrong person. The risk is real, but nevertheless learning to tell the truth and to trust others is essential in re-covery. How else can people help us? I've given my trust to my family and closest friends. I had been afraid of hurting them with my pain. I still don't want to do that, but I owe them the truth, and I need to tell it to them. Once I couldn't get the words out; now I can. Knowing how things really are with me helps them hold me up when depression is sucking me down. Over time I've learned to trust colleagues and a wide circle of friends. They're human. They have occasionally let me down, but most of the time I've been right to trust them.

I've also extended my trust to the mental health professionals I've worked with, and my recovery has benefited. I have friends living with a mental illness who have regretted trusting a particular therapist or psychia-trist. From their experience, I encourage you to learn all that you can about the professionals you are working with. Ask questions, test the waters, and give your trust only when it feels safe to do so. Don't give up. Finding a professional you can fully trust is vital to recovery.

If I hadn't trusted that the cataract surgeon wouldn't pop my eyeball out, my vision in that eye would pretty much be gone by now. If I hadn't trusted other people, my life would be far less satisfying than it is now. In fact, I'm not sure that I would have much of a life at all. There are risks to trusting, but there are ways we can limit those risks. Nevertheless, I sim-ply do not believe that it is possible to recover from mental illness without trusting other people.

HELP 4

Recovering Self-Worth

WHAT AM I WORTH? In the worst times of my depression, the answer came quickly: "Not much." Depression leeches away self-worth until you feel that your life has negative value. Do the math and you can say, "I am a subtraction from the net value of the universe." This is the technical way of saying, "I'm a piece of shit." When you feel this way, it's hard to summon up much energy to work on recovery. Why bother? It's much easier to push the button and hear the flush, the sound of your own worthlessness. Hard words and a crude image, but they are the absolute truth of what depression does to your self-worth.

By denying that we have value, depression lies to us. I have a huge basket full of all the cards that members of my church, including many children, sent me while I was in the hospital for my mental illness. In so many ways, they told me that they cared about me, missed me, and wished me a speedy recovery. Many thanked me for helping them, and some included stories about how my help had been essential in their getting through difficult times in their lives. In the face of all this evidence to the contrary, how could I possibly think that I have no value?

Following my second hospitalization and two failed attempts to return to my church, I knew my recovery required that I resign as minister after serving more than twenty-five years. The church hosted a celebration of gratitude for me, where I was told again and again—in person and in an enormous scrapbook—how much my ministry had meant to them. I came away from that celebration with a powerful feeling of being loved. Again, how can I possibly think that I have no value?

But depression holds on tight as long as it can. Depression told me that people wrote nice things only because they had fallen for the one skill I really had: telling lies. If they only knew the truth about me, they'd give me the contempt I deserved. Slowly, sometimes having to cover the same ground over and over, my therapist helped me stop listening to my depression. Depression was the liar, not me. My therapist helped me receive the words and deeds of my parishioners as gifts of gratitude and love, as nourishment for my self-worth and self-esteem.

I believe the heart of the recovery of one's self-worth is this realization that you are loved and cared about. Even though depression turned my life into hell, it could never completely take away my belief that my wife and children loved me. True, depression easily convinced me I didn't deserve their love and tried hard to convince me they would be better off without me, but the reality of their love was too strong. In therapy I was able to recognize depression's lies and to fully savor the love that is mine. My self-worth thrives when I know I'm loved. I believe this is true for us all. It is the way we are wired as human beings.

For many, recovery of self-worth is also enhanced by religious tradition. For example, in Psalm 8, we are told that we are made only a "little lower than the angels" and that we are crowned "with glory and honor." I memorized this psalm a long time ago, and I still turn to it when life has given my self-worth a hit. If its words speak truth to you, then you have a powerful ally in your recovery. Likewise, if you share my own faith tradition, understanding Jesus as God's gift of love to us, then your self-worth is underwritten by this divine act.

There are also powerful assertions of human value outside of faith traditions. The arts in all their forms—wherever human creativity flourishes—are statement of our value and worth. Athletes, who for a moment suspend gravity, leave us agape in awe. This computer on which I am typing is a product of human creativity and ingenuity beyond what anyone would have dreamed only a few years ago. We've been to the moon and unlocked the genome. We create wonder.

The awesome and the wonderful inspire us, but it is the everyday that sustains us. Once depression's grip on my life was broken, I found a kind of daily nourishment in small things. If somebody says thank you, I feel like a deposit has been made in my self-worth account. When I get a good night's sleep, I wake up feeling more valuable. Add a good breakfast, especially if there's bacon, and that feeling intensifies. If I'm lucky, the day ends with a spectacular sunset. I savor it, feeling as if some of that indescribable beauty is seeping into me. I can't argue the logic of why any of this is the case; I just know that it is.

Assertions of self-worth can be found in unexpected places, as in this story from Memphis, Tennessee. On July 18, 1953, Elvis Presley went into Sun Records studio in that city. He paid $3.98 to record the first of two double-sided demos. In the version of the story I heard, the assistant who was setting voice levels asked him, "What kind of singer are you?" "I sing all kinds." The assistant tried again, "Who do you sound like?" Elvis responded with God's honest truth: "I don't sound like nobody."

He got that right, and what's true of Elvis is true of you and me. Nobody sounds like nobody because we're all unique. Sounding like nobody can help us in the recovery of self-worth. Imagine Elvis at the Sun Records studio going on to say something like, "Yep, I don't sound like nobody, and I don't need to sound like nobody. I sound just fine the way I am, so turn on that recording machine I'm paying good money for."

There are two recovery lessons here. First, Elvis helps us understand that each of us is unique and our uniqueness is valuable. He said, "I don't sound like nobody." If Elvis hadn't made that recording, something irreplaceable would have been lost, something of unlimited value would not exist. Second, Elvis wants us to recognize that in whatever way each of us is unique—well, that's just fine. This is a lesson in self-acceptance, and self-acceptance is a first cousin to self-worth. Elvis was just fine with being Elvis. Such is our goal in recovery—OK, not for us to be fine being Elvis, though I guess you could be an impersonator. The goal of recovery is for each of us to be just fine being who we are. When you feel this way, your self-worth will soar.

Maybe this sounds too good to be true, so let's test it with some reality. I know that I'm not as successful as A, not as smart as B, and not as handsome as C (though I think C is dying his hair). In fact, I can go from A to Z over and over again finding people who are superior to me in some way. But, not to worry: I don't sound like nobody. My life is unique, a one-off in the universe, irreplaceable and invaluable. I'm almost up there with the angels. And you know what else? There are people who love me just as I am right now. This is my truth, so much stronger than depression's lie.

Help 5

Celebrating Myself

CELEBRATING OUR ACCOMPLISHMENTS IS another way we can enhance our self-worth. Whereas depression would have us discount our successes and minimize all we've done that's good, in recovery we learn to fully savor our accomplishments. This is what I've learned to do with that basket full of all the cards that expressed the gratitude of my parishioners.

Another kind of success came when I started the hospital day program after my first hospitalization. The first two mornings my wife Susan drove me from home to the hospital and then picked me up when the program ended for the day. We never talked about this, but we both knew why. My suicidal thoughts had gathered around crashing the car into a tree, specifically the big elm at the end of our block. One step at a time felt right—first the program, later the driving.

The third morning I said that I would drive myself, and she agreed. I don't remember a big struggle about this, only that I was now far from feeling suicidal and that it felt normal to drive myself. Driving back and forth to the hospital turned out to be a nonevent. Maybe I was a little more careful and attentive than usual, but that was about it. I remember listening to a Nora Jones CD as I drove. When she sang about the river sheltering her, I felt that she was singing to me.

The next day I again drove myself. On the way home, I stopped at my favorite coffee shop for an almond scone and a cup of coffee, the blend that they called "Mississippi mud." Coffee and a scone isn't what I usually have late in the afternoon, but I needed to celebrate being able to drive myself without fear. I had accomplished something, my recovery had moved forward, and I deserved a celebration.

In the months that followed, my therapist made it a point to celebrate whenever he believed that we'd reached a milestone in our work together. He didn't buy me a scone and a cup of Mississippi mud, but he did point out that it isn't easy to talk about what hurts, that it takes courage to open up about what was taboo for so long, and that making fundamental changes in one's life is hard work. I deeply appreciated his recognition of what I had done, and I felt better about myself because of it.

Can there be any doubt about how beneficial celebrations like this are for a person's recovery? I don't think so, but my personal history intrudes into the celebration. Raised in a family where the approval of my parents was based on achievement and success, I became an adult who needed to achieve more and more to feel good about myself. If there's such a thing as achievement addiction, I could be its poster child.

It's a quandary: I want to celebrate my successes, and I need to celebrate them, but success as a necessity for self-worth has played a major role in my mental illness. How do I sort this out? In recovery I've learned to get help when faced with such a question, usually by talking with someone I trust, but sometimes help has come from an unexpected source. An example of this comes from *Cool Runnings*, a movie about the Jamaican Olympic bobsled team. In the movie, a disgraced Olympian (who was stripped of his gold medal because he had cheated in the bobsled competition years before) becomes the unlikely coach of an unlikely team, as Jamaica is not exactly known as a powerhouse in winter sports. In a pivotal scene, Derice (Leon), a team member, asks Irv (John Candy), the coach, a difficult question.

Derice: Hey, Coach.

Irv: Yeah?

Derice: I have to ask you a question.

Irv: Sure.

Derice: But you don't have to answer if you don't want to. I mean, I want you to, but if you can't, I understand.

Irv: You wanna know why I cheated, right?

Derice: Yes, I do.

Irv: That's a fair question. It's quite simple, really. I had to win. You see, Derice, I'd made winning my whole life. And when you make winning your whole life, you have to keep on winning, no matter what. You understand that?

Derice: No, I don't understand. You won two gold medals. You had it all.

Irv: Derice, a gold medal is a wonderful thing. But if you're not enough without one, you'll never be enough with one.[3]

15

A gold medal is a wonderful thing, worthy of the sacrifice required to win it. But even such a singular achievement will not sustain a person's life. As Irv says, it's still not enough. The only reality adequate to our need, the one that makes us big enough, is our own life.

In "Song of Myself," Walt Whitman, poet of life, celebrates us all.

> I celebrate myself,
> And what I assume you shall assume,
> For every atom belonging to me as good belongs to you.
>
> I loafe and invite my soul,
> I lean and loafe at my ease . . . . observing a spear of summer grass.[4]

These verses overflow with the joy of self-acceptance. In opposition to a world of ever-intensifying demands and pressure to achieve, the poet loafs and invites his ease. He knows that one doesn't need to accomplish or achieve anything to enjoy life or to feel good about oneself. Self-worth comes with the package of being human. Why knock yourself out for what is already yours as a birthright? Maybe the most essential words for one in recovery are "I celebrate myself." That's it.

Whitman is in no way exclusive or jealous in his self-celebration. He tells us that we are made of the same stuff as he and that we have just as much reason to celebrate. There's nothing we have to do; we have all we need. So lean back, relax, and take time to observe a spear of summer grass. You won't know how beautiful it is until you take time to really look at it. Loaf, enjoy the day and the beauty right in front of your nose. You'll feel like a million bucks.

Another quote from "Song of Myself":

> Do I contradict myself?
> Very well then . . . . I contradict myself,
> I am large . . . . I contain multitudes.[5]

Whitman is an ecstatic, celebrating life that forever overflows words, logic, and boundaries. If his thinking changes, well, life changes. Life is a river, not a monument. Whatever I am today, I will be different tomorrow. Words can't begin to capture all of me. I'm so much more than labels or categories—or a diagnosis, for that matter. I'm also so much more than any achievement. Of course, I'll celebrate each success, and I invite you to do the same. Like blades of grass, they're wonderful. But I don't have to have them. You see, I already have enough. "I celebrate myself."

Help 6

Asking for What You Want

SOMETIMES IN RECOVERY WE need to learn new things, and sometimes we need to unlearn old ones. I've needed to unlearn rules I was taught in childhood, such as always keeping my real feelings and desires carefully hidden where nobody could find them. Following this rule has made it hard for me to ask for help, and unlearning it has been an ongoing work in my recovery.

Compare this self-defeating rule I learned as a child in Virginia to the rule I learned as an adult in Minnesota, what we call "Minnesota Nice." Here's an example, maybe slightly exaggerated, from an everyday "Minnesota Nice" social exchange.

Sven has dropped by Ole and Lena's to return their ice auger. Of course Lena invites him in and says:

"How about a cup of coffee?"

"Oh, no thanks, Lena. No need for you to go to so much trouble."

"No trouble at all. Take the load off, and I'll bring you some in our brand-new Minnesota Vikings mug."

"Well, maybe, if you have some of yesterday's, I could use it up for you. No need to heat it up. I like it tepid."

"No trouble, Sven. I made some fresh. How about one of these rhubarb bars?"

"I can't take your rhubarb bars. I know you and Ole love your rhubarb."

"You got that right. But we got more than enough for us. You'd be helping us out if you ate some."

"Are you sure?"

"You betcha!"

"Well, whatever. If you put it like that, I guess maybe I'll have half a bar. But no ice cream on it. I don't want you to go to any more trouble. You've gone to too much trouble already."

"No trouble, and you can't have rhubarb without ice cream. I'll run down to the store and be back in a jiffy. I've got the coupon right here."

Minnesota Nice pretty much operates by the same unwritten rules I learned as a child: 1) Never say honestly how you feel. 2) Never say directly what you want. In my experience as a long-term resident, we Minnesotans use Minnesota Nice to make gentle fun of ourselves as much as we use it to get coffee and rhubarb bars. Watch two skilled natives following the rules of Minnesota Nice, and you'll see how closely they flirt with self-parody while keeping a straight face.

But Minnesota Nice has a limit. With its proximity to parody, it works only when there's not much at stake. This is where Minnesota Nice differs from the rules I learned long ago in Virginia. As a child, everything was at stake for me. I was forming the basics of how I operated as a human being, how to meet my deepest needs in my relationships with other people. During this vulnerable time, I learned rules that have damaged my life.

This became clear on my first posthospitalization visit with a therapist. Following some introductions, he got me a cup of coffee. Then I started telling him what I hoped were some mildly entertaining stories about my life as a minister, keeping my feelings and wants well out of the stories. He listened but didn't say much. If he had followed the rule of never saying directly how one felt, he should have told me some mildly entertaining stories of his life as a therapist, passing the time and keeping all his feelings and genuine wants safely hidden. He didn't play by this rule. Instead, he left it up to me to keep the safe conversation going.

Unfortunately (or, perhaps, fortunately) I didn't have fifty minutes of mildly entertaining stories, and besides I was still pretty blitzed from being in the hospital. As things dragged on, I sneaked a look at the clock on his bookcase. Either it was broken or I was going to run out of nice talk long before the session ended. Finally I couldn't think of anything more to say. I panicked, apologized to my therapist, and told him how sorry I was for being boring and wasting his time. For the first time in the session, I had told him the truth about how I felt. He asked me why I thought I was wasting his time.

At that moment we began our work together. Before long we were talking about feelings: the hurt, shame, and fear that I'd learned not to talk about as a child. He taught me that by following the rule of keeping my feelings hidden, I had vastly increased the power of those feelings to hurt me. From then until now, I've been working hard to unlearn that rule.

I've also been working hard to unlearn the rule about not asking directly for what I want. For so long, I expected family members and friends to read my mind. I expected them to know what I wanted without my saying a word about it. I would become irritated when someone didn't do what I'd never asked them to do.

In my work at church, I did something similar, creating a web of unspoken agreements designed to get my needs met without ever directly saying what I wanted. It went something like this: *I'm going to work really hard for you. I'm going to keep the church growing. I will keep it in good financial shape for you. I'm going to give you nothing to complain about, because I'm going to anticipate all of your wants and desires. And you, in fair return for my niceness and hard work, will be nice to me, never hassle me, go along with my ideas, and tell me regularly that I am doing a good job.*

In his book *Feeling Good*, David Burns discusses Margaret, a patient whose behavior throws light on my own. "She applied this rule to all human relationships. 'If I do nice things for people they *should* reciprocate.'"[6] This sounds reasonable, but actually it's not reasonable at all. As Burns writes, "She went around always doing good things for her husband and others and then waited for their reciprocity. Unfortunately, these unilateral contracts fell apart because other people usually weren't aware that she expected to be repaid."[7]

As with Margaret, my "unilateral contracts" were not repaid. I was constantly setting myself up to be surprised and disappointed when people didn't do what they didn't know they'd agreed to do. The agreement was all in my head. It's taken a lot of work to see what I'd been doing, to be able to talk about it, and to stop doing it.

In my recovery I'm learning to live honestly, which for me means simply saying how I feel and asking for what I want. No more "unilateral contracts" and no more manipulation. I'm still working on living honestly, but I've learned to enjoy being a straightforward person. So pass me the damn rhubarb bars and slather on the ice cream.

Help 7

Recovering Humor

I CAN ONLY TALK about painful things for so long, and I suspect you're the same way. At the heart of this book is my story of living with mental illness. I work hard to tell the story honestly, which at times means that telling my story can be painful. After a while, I have to back away from it. I need a break, and the best break is something that makes me laugh. Besides providing a break, humor can be a way to tell the truth about ourselves and to keep things in perspective.

I have a friend who describes herself as a "high-functioning depressive." This phrase allows her to put several truths together. She is indeed high functioning and very good at a demanding job. She's also modest and self-effacing. I don't think she could tell you that she's good at her work except by using language that's self-deprecating. She's also someone who lives with depression. The phrase *high-functioning depressive* allows her to speak of her illness in a way that's comfortable for her. To paraphrase Emily Dickinson, she tells all the truth, but she tells it slant.

I can look forward to laughter when I'm with this friend, but I wasn't expecting to find laughter at one of my earliest sessions with my therapist. I was waiting for him to bring me a cup of coffee. Offering me a cup of coffee was how he started each session, a simple act of kindness that did much to cement our relationship.

While I waited, I read the titles of some of the books on his bookshelf. I don't remember them, but I do remember that if you put them all together, you'd have a list of every mental dysfunction that's befallen humankind since Adam, Eve, and the serpent. It was a bookshelf of doom; demons were flying out of those books. My thoughts went something like: *OK, I know I'm sick, but I can't have all this stuff wrong with me. No way. You've got to be kidding.* The book titles were so over-the-top that I couldn't help but laugh. Just then he came in with my coffee. I'll always wonder what he thought of me sitting there laughing alone, though I'm sure there's an explanation for it in one of his books.

When going into the therapist's office, my dominant feelings were shame and fear. My meds were making me feel like a stranger to my own mind. Though he had reassured me otherwise, I still feared that my therapist would tell me my problems were tedious and boring, a waste of his professional time. I could barely keep it all together, yet the bookcase full of doom struck me as funny. Something about being able to laugh in that place gave me hope that the therapy was going to be OK. Humor is wonderfully resilient.

Finding some humor in a situation allows you to step back and see things more clearly. Laughing is like taking a deep breath and bringing everything back down to earth. *Relax, this therapist just brought me a cup of coffee. He's not going to kick me out after a couple of sessions, even if his choices of reading matter are a little off-putting.*

This feeling reminds me of watching movies on the psych unit with other patients, laughing hard at the best lines and funniest scenes. One night we were watching *Tootsie* together and came to the part where someone suggests that Tootsie go see a therapist. The audience howled, and some of them attacked the screen with a barrage of popcorn, simultaneously letting loose in graphic language, saying exactly what they thought of one therapist or another. Locked in that place with no control over what would happen next, we could laugh, which meant we had some control after all.

I cannot write about using humor in recovery without a caution. Humor can help in many ways; it can also do harm. It's like fire—it's good or bad depending upon how it's used. There's a kind of humor that allows the truth to be told, but there's also sarcasm that inflicts pain. Unacknowledged anger at another person can easily sneak out through sarcasm. I do my best not to do that, but if it happens, I do my best to apologize.

This same caution applies when I direct humor inward. When I laugh at depression's machinations, I move my recovery along. For example, sometimes I catch myself catastrophizing in several mutually contradictory directions at once. Just when I'm thinking, *Nobody likes me*, I'm also thinking, *People just won't stop calling me because they want me to do stuff with them*. Then I laugh at what I'm doing. When my wife asks me to do something new, I reflexively say no, a puff of automatic anxiety. Then we both smile, because we know that saying no is just what I do. Give me a moment, and I may change the no to a yes: I'm happy to go to that new lutefisk restaurant after all. (For non-Minnesotans, lutefisk is codfish that has been dried and then reconstituted. Depending on your taste, it's heavenly or it's fish Jell-O.) When I catch myself brooding about my life being nothing but a sea of troubles, I remember what a girlfriend called me in high school: "Woeful Wobert." It always makes me smile.

Sometimes I've laughed at myself with contempt and fierce anger. This doesn't happen so much anymore, but I'm still capable of it. I have to pay attention to what I'm laughing at. Humor can be a way to take depression down a peg, a way to tell the truth, and a way to cope. However, if misused, it can be a way to hurt others and oneself. I use humor because I need every tool available to help me in recovery. It can be a very good tool, though it's also a sharp one.

I think that the best humor keeps us grounded. There is a relationship between human, humor, and humus. The best humor lets us laugh at everything that would deny our humanity, including the absurd demands we sometimes make on ourselves. It brings us back down to earth, literally to the soil, the humus. On that early visit to my therapist, I was a new client with huge anxieties. He had all the power, but he also had a library full of strange books. I laughed and suddenly the distance between us closed, and my feet were on solid ground.

HELP 8

Structuring Each Day

FOR MORE THAN FOURTEEN years now, each day after I have finished break-fast, I take my second or maybe third cup of coffee to my study, a pretentious title for the ex-bedroom of one of our kids. I sit down in a big blue recliner, the gift of a former parishioner who was downsizing, and pick up my copy of *The Book of Common Prayer* from the Episcopal Church and a very tat-tered Bible. In the back of the prayer book, there's a two-year cycle of daily scripture readings called the Daily Office Lectionary. I find the reading for that day, put a check mark by the date in the lectionary, and then read the assigned scripture. The whole process takes me maybe fifteen minutes.

When I first started reading scripture each morning, I was often unable to focus on the book in front of me. Medications, my recent hospitalization, the raging of my depression—I don't know all the reasons, but I do know I could have been reading Klingon or Elvish for all that I understood. Still, and this was critical at that time in my recovery, I could take my sharpened pencil and put that little check mark next to the right date in the lectionary.

These little check marks, which gradually became a great multitude of check marks, showed that I had accomplished something. There was no denying that I had turned to these passages and at least looked at them for a time. Many days looking at the passages was my sole accomplishment. Yet even this small act meant a lot, my first experience of celebrating achieve-ments in recovery. It's the inspiration for the short chapters in this book, short enough to read a chapter even on a bad day. Doing a little is so much better than doing nothing.

In the first months of my recovery, this simple truth was brought home to me on a daily basis: I'm up, I've had breakfast, the nest is empty, and I don't have a job. What do I do with my day? Well, first I'm going to gather up my Bible, my *Book of Common Prayer*, and my cup of coffee. Then I'm going to read the passages for today. There's some order to my life, and this is deeply calming. Of course, there's still most of the day ahead of me with time to fill and decisions to be made. We'll see how all that goes, but right now, I don't have to think about it or decide anything. I have something to do, a simple plan, and somehow this settles me down in a way that makes it easier to put the rest of the day together.

I've been doing it for fourteen years. As my recovery has progressed, I have been fortunate to find other ways to order my life beyond my scripture reading and check marks. But most days I remain faithful to this practice, a calming deep breath at the start of the day. It reminds me of how far I have come and helps me remember not to take this progress for granted. Besides, when my depression intensifies, there are days when I once again need the reassurance of having something structured to do. It is a way to push back against depression's inertia and disorganization.

I invite you to consider doing something similar to my daily practice. If scripture reading is not the right one for you, there are many other possibilities. Read something that enriches your life—a spiritual guide, a book of Helps for recovery from mental illness (and recommend the book to your friends!), poetry, a classic, or simply a book you like. Meditation or yoga could be your daily practice; so could listening to music, painting, or knitting. Journaling can be both a daily practice and a way to push back against depression. There are so many options. Pick whatever works for you.

Given how I've been helped by keeping a record of my daily readings (all those check marks), I suggest you find some way of keeping a tangible record of whatever you choose as your daily practice. On a bad day, you can look at it and have proof that you've accomplished something. Giving yourself some credit is a good exercise in countering the incessant self-criticism of depression.

In addition to what we choose to do each day, there are other daily practices, so obvious that it's easy to overlook them. In *Acedia & Me*, Kathleen Norris describes daily routines such as taking a shower, popping a multivitamin, and making your bed as acts of hospitality and respect toward oneself.[8] We usually think of these tasks as chores, something best to get over with. Norris is asking us to stop and reframe our thinking, to see these routines as significant daily practices. These acts of hospitality are a sign of our self-worth, gifts that we give ourselves because we deserve them.

Recovery is supported by these acts of self-hospitality. They counter the damage mental illness does to our self-worth and self-respect. When we recognize these acts as gifts to ourselves, we are repairing this damage. They are daily acts; like the check marks, their power is cumulative. Over time, they become a strong reassurance of our value as human beings.

If we repeat these acts often enough and long enough, they become habits. Sometimes habits are thought of as things we do without thinking, but that's not what I mean. I'm thinking of habits in terms of my daily scripture reading, as something we do regularly that calms us and makes it easier for us to decide what to do next. Mental illness has swept us through a turbulent time where the unpredictable and the unexpected have become our normal. It has taken us to a place that's strange and made us strangers to ourselves. Things that we used to count on, including things in our own minds, aren't the same anymore. How can we move ahead when we have no idea what we can rely upon?

In the face of this uncertainty, habits give us at least a small area of control. Reading the scripture each morning is something I can rely on, a little bit of high ground amidst the flood. It's a start in recovery and proof that not everything is always changing. I know what I'm going to be doing tomorrow, because it's what I do every day.

HELP 9

Dealing with Expectations

ONE OF MY FAVORITE lines in the movie *Raising Arizona* comes when Evelle Snoats (John Goodman) asks the unemployed hero H.I. McDunnough (Nicholas Cage) a question, "H.I., you're young and you got your health, what you want with a job?"[9] It's a perfect non sequitur. You think that Evelle Snoats is going to give the unemployed H.I. a job-hunting pep talk. Instead you get the exact opposite—"What you want with a job?"

If you're young and healthy, then you go get a job. That's the societal expectation, and it slips on a banana peel thanks to Mr. Snoats. I love to see expectations fall on their butt; high expectations have caused me so much pain. I've told you I could be the poster boy for achievement addiction. This is largely the result of my parents' expectation, especially my dad's, that I would accomplish great things. I learned that his affection was contingent on my meeting his expectations. I believe that my dad was parenting me the same way he had been parented and that this contributed to the mental illness of two of his sisters. Who knows how many generations this toxic parenting style was passed down through his family?

My dad died more than thirty years ago, but his expectations stayed alive in my mind. I expected success and needed incontrovertible proof of that success. For a while in college, graduate school, and seminary, I was able to meet these expectations with good grades at prestigious schools. My first call was as an associate minister at a large flourishing church, another demonstrable success, and I continued to stay on track in meeting expectations.

Then I moved on to be the solo pastor at a small church with money troubles and deferred building maintenance. Over time the church did grow and the finances got better, but the expectations I had internalized were far from satisfied. Success, if it was happening at all, didn't have the wonderful tangibility of a report card full of A's or a position at a large impressive-looking church. Failing to meet expectations, I became a harsh and unforgiving critic of myself, and my self-esteem plummeted.

I also suspected that others were aware that I wasn't measuring up and that they were beginning to wonder whether they'd made the right decision in hiring me. I doubted if they even took me and my work seriously. Maybe my minuscule accomplishments were some kind of joke to them. I felt awful, and the awful that I felt was shame. Looking back, in reality I'm not sure even one person in the church had such a negative opinion of my work, but I wasn't dealing with reality.

In *I Thought It Was Just Me (but it isn't)*, Dr. Brené Brown describes shame as something operating like the lens of a camera that zooms in on you so your flawed self, alone and struggling, is in sharp focus for all to see.[10] For me the camera was rolling 24/7, and people were starting to laugh.

As with so much in recovery, overcoming expectations and shame began while I was on the psych unit. I was there with other patients, and soon I struck up friendships with some of them. We sat together at the nightly movies, made it a point to have meals together, made eye contact during group therapy, and made poop jokes together on one wonderful occasion about which dogs were sure to defecate during pet therapy.

No big deal, we were simply friends facing together what life was bringing us in that strange place. But in truth, it was a big deal. It was an example of what Dr. Brown describes as zooming out:

> When we zoom out, we start to see a completely different picture.
> We see many people in the same struggle. Rather than thinking,
> "I'm the only one," we start thinking, "I can't believe it! You too?
> I'm normal? I thought it was just me!"[11]

The camera zoomed out for me on the psych unit. The other patients and I were in the same struggle; it certainly wasn't just me. Given that we were in a psych unit, I couldn't exactly say, "I'm normal." But in this context, I fit right in. Far from isolated, I was part of a makeshift community who did all sorts of things together. Though I wish it had, this zooming out of the camera didn't make my shame totally disappear, but it did shrink the shame down some.

In the years since I finally was able to return to work, I have tried to keep the camera from once again zooming in on me. Instead of focusing on myself, I have learned to work with others to create a group expectation for what needed to be done for the best interest of all. When we failed, it wasn't just me that failed; I wasn't isolated. And when we succeeded, the celebration was for all of us. This is a lesson in teamwork that I suspect many people learn long before they are old enough to be card-carrying AARP members. I wish I had learned it much earlier in my own life, but I am grateful that I learned it when I did.

This learning has also figured in how I can find support from colleagues. The congregations I've served aren't facing their problems in isolation. We're dealing with trends in churches and society; we're all in it together. Hence other clergy and I are a natural support group for one another, and I regularly seek to be with groups of colleagues who share these problems with me. When we are able to trust one another and share the stories of our day-to-day struggles, we have a powerful antidote to isolation and shame. Together we learn to scale our expectations of ourselves and our churches back to reality. If—in your profession or in any other part of your life—you are facing problems that you know others are confronting, I hope that you can find a group so you will experience the kind of support I have found.

As I have learned more about expectations and the shame that they cause, I've increasingly been able to let go of the harmful expectations I learned as a child. I've learned that it's actually OK to have expectations of oneself, as long as they really are your own, as long as they are expectations that you have intentionally and freely chosen. For example, the friendships I have made in my years of recovery are important to me, and I want to be a good and loyal friend in return. This is now an expectation I have of myself, and I try to achieve it to the best of my ability. When I do, I feel good about myself, and my self-worth benefits. This is such a different feeling from the emotion I've felt when trying to meet the expectations of someone else. Striving to meet the expectations of others has left me looking over my shoulder, wondering whether I really did well enough—and already dreading the next more-demanding expectation.

Another example: people who know about my illness often come to me with their own mental health questions, especially questions about depression. Of course, I can't answer every question, but I expect myself to listen carefully to each one, to take whatever time is required to respond, and to try to respond honestly from my own experience and from the experiences of others. I'll be as open as I can about what I don't know, what I'm unsure of, and what I'm conflicted about. Finally, if appropriate, I'll do my best to point them toward some resource or some person more able than I to answer a particular question. As I expect myself to be a loyal friend, I expect myself to be a good support for others living with mental illness.

Like celebrating success, there's a place in recovery to celebrate meeting expectations. When those expectations are the ones my folks drilled into me, the ones that have caused me so much pain, I hope that they will slip on a banana peel and land really hard. But when they are truly my own expectations, especially when they involve friendship and caring about other people, then they are allies in drawing me out of isolation and in increasing my self-worth. If one of my own expectations drew close to a banana peel, I'd snatch that peel away as quickly as possible.

HELP 10

Exercising, Telling Stories, and Drumming

FOR VARIETY AND A bit of a respite, I've included some short pieces like this one as part of the Forty-Nine Helps.

GET SOME REGULAR EXERCISE

My doctor on the psych unit told me that I was "burning up with adrenalin" and that I should start exercising regularly to diminish the adrenalin and other stress hormones. He didn't care so much about what kind of exercise I chose, only that I give it at least thirty minutes and that I do it most days. I've chosen walking. Running, swimming, yoga, or working out in the gym would give me more exercise benefit and burn off more stress-inducing hormones. But walking is my speed, I keep at it, and it's done a lot to improve my overall health as well as my sense of well-being.

Especially early in my recovery, when my self-worth was minimal and the days felt very long, taking a walk, like reading daily scripture, helped structure my time and give me a sense of accomplishment. Over time I've found a variety of other benefits from regular walks: I've struck up conversations with other walkers, learned about dog breeds and been invited to pet all kinds of dogs, listened to birds and seen some magnificent ones, seen a fox and some albino squirrels, enjoyed watching the flowers come and go—a sign of the changing seasons, which alternate with the coming and going of the snowbanks. Best of all I've found dropped coins and, on one memorable occasion, a ten-dollar bill. Now every one of my walks is a hunt for free-range money, adding pleasure to regular exercise.

I recommend that you try walking, but it really doesn't matter what exercise you choose. What matters is all the benefits that accrue from regularly caring for your body. As you are able, I encourage you to find the exercise that is most satisfying and doable for you. If you do pick walking, especially if you walk in Minnesota in the early spring, keep your eyes on the edges of receding snowbanks. Coins dropped in the winter become treasures found in the spring.

TELL STORIES

While in recovery, some stories have become treasures for me. They tell the truth. They are not just words, but something tangible and real. For example, I have a story about baptizing a particularly cute baby in my first parish. Her proud parents and godparents were standing next to me, and the congregation was all smiles and blessings. As I held the baby and said the sacred words, the joy in the sanctuary was palpable; new life was in our midst. Yet I had a problem saying the holy words clearly and distinctly, because the beloved child kept sticking her right index finger deeper and deeper into my left nostril. Whenever I get a little too rigid or overly caught up in my role as a pastor, remembering this baby and her wandering finger makes me smile and brings me back down to earth.

Another of my favorite stories is from *Salvation on Sand Mountain* by Denis Covington, in which he describes his experience in churches where serpents are sometimes handled during worship. Covington asks Uncle Ully Lynn what it's like to take up a serpent. Uncle Ully answers, "You're in a prayerful state. You can't have your mind on other things. The Spirit tells you what to do."[12]

You can bet the farm on it: I'll never handle a serpent while having my mind on other things. Put the snake in my hand, let me feel it writhe a little between my fingers, and you can count on my undivided attention. Try this yourself as a mental exercise, and you'll see what I mean. I tell this story, not to promote snake handling in churches, but to promote paying attention to external reality. If we want to live fully, enjoy all that is good in life, then we can't have our minds on other things.

Another favorite story—I don't remember where I heard it—speaks truth to depression's lies. It's about a school that was built by volunteers in a Nicaraguan village. To gauge the school's impact on all the villagers, an old woman who had spent her whole life there was asked what she thought of it. She said that she was excited about the education children would receive, beginning with how they would learn to read and write. Somebody then asked her whether she could read. She pointed to the school, smiled broadly, and said, "Not yet."

I know what depression has cost me, and I acknowledge its power. But what it did to me in the past doesn't have to limit my future. I've learned vital lessons in recovery and found the support I needed; now I am moving into a future unspoiled by depression. With these thoughts, I smile like the woman in the story and think of the good things in life that I still want to experience.

FINDING A DRUM

I have a friend living with mental illness who is part of several drumming circles. For him the sound of the drum is so absorbing that it drives away his depression. One of his teachers, a Native American, told him that the drum is the heartbeat of the earth. This heartbeat takes my friend to a place where depression can't follow. I've looked for something like my friend's drumming that can fully absorb my own attention. The closest I've come is what I'm doing now. Writing can blot out the rest of the world for me, so absorb my attention that I have none to give to anything else, including depression.

I invite you to find what absorbs your attention, like drumming for my friend and writing for me. Many people find it in music and art, but it could be anything from repairing bicycles to working out. I've heard people talk about their favorite TV series with a passion that made it clear they were totally absorbed in it. Some people get lost in a book, and others get lost in a conversation with a close friend. Travel can totally absorb a person's attention, so can a baseball game. There are so many kinds of drums. You'll know yours when it takes you to a place where depression can't follow.

HELP 11

Escaping Perfectionism

I ONCE OFFICIATED AT a funeral for a guinea pig named Flashlight, the class pet for a kindergartner in the church I served for so long. As Flashlight had left no will or funeral instructions, I did not know any favorite hymns or Bible verses. I did know that Flashlight had been "a good guinea pig," so I used that idea as the center of the eulogy. No decisions had been made about donations in lieu of flowers, but the family had decided to have carrot cake at the post-funeral reception, an appropriate tribute to Flashlight, who loved carrots.

At the appointed time, my young parishioner, his parents, his kindergarten teacher, a few neighbors, and I gathered for the backyard graveside service. I invited those in attendance to share reminiscences of Flashlight's life, and then I led them in a prayer of thanksgiving for the departed.

As I gave the eulogy for Flashlight, I talked about the joy Flashlight had brought to the family and about the love pets bring into our lives. I did my best. But, as the eulogy went on, I realized that I had failed to ask the family one crucial question before the funeral: was Flashlight male or female? Because I hadn't asked, I didn't know which pronoun to use in referring to Flashlight, so I just kept saying "Flashlight." I was sure that people noticed and that they knew I had not done my homework on Flashlight's behalf.

After the service, over generous slices of carrot cake, the kindergartner with tears in his eyes thanked me for what I'd said about Flashlight. His parents also thanked me and told me how grateful they were that I had taken so much time for their son. No one mentioned the lack of pronouns, though I was sure it had to be what everybody was thinking about. In Minnesota people try to be nice, at least nice to the minister after a funeral. But they knew.

Over the years, whenever I thought about this service, I ended up dwelling on how I hadn't asked whether Flashlight was male or female and how my failure had spoiled the funeral. Finally in a conversation with the parents many years later, I fessed up about how bad I felt for not asking. They couldn't believe that it bothered me. "Bob," the boy's mother exclaimed, "none of us knew whether Flashlight was a boy or a girl. Who can tell with a guinea pig? You'd need a vet. We were just so grateful you took time out of your busy schedule to do this for our son. It meant a lot to him and to us."

What does this funeral and my reaction to it have to do with depression? Everything. Depression spoils things. A little boy had given me his trust, honored me as his minister. His parents were grateful then and they were still grateful years later. There was so much for me to feel good about, and yet, because of depression, I'd let one mistake (which turned out not even to be a mistake) spoil it all. Instead of savoring what I had done, I was beating myself up about my public failure. Instead of satisfaction, I was left with shame.

Depression is so good at doing this, at seeking out the least little pieces of negativity in any situation. Like a hungry chicken pecking in the dirt for dried-up corn, depression takes whatever joy it can find and snatches it up. Then by some kind of perverse magic, depression causes this little piece of negativity to balloon in size until there is no room left in your mind for anything else.

David Burns uses the cognitive behavioral therapy term "mental filter"[13] to describe how negativity can overwhelm one's thoughts. He writes, "You pick out a negative detail in any situation and dwell on it exclusively, thus perceiving that the whole situation is negative."[14] This describes what I had done: I used not knowing the right pronoun as the negative detail to spoil what was actually quite wonderful.

Like a guinea pig hiding in tall grass, perfectionism lurked behind my mental filtering. Since Flashlight's service wasn't perfect, or so I thought, I didn't think that there was anything at all good about the event. The time I'd spent didn't matter; the families' gratitude didn't matter; the honor a little boy had given me didn't matter. I'd failed, and that's all there was to it. Like the magical ballooning of tiny negatives in mental filtering, none of this has anything to do with reality. Even if I had made a mistake, I'd gotten many things right, indeed the most important things. But perfectionism would give me credit for nothing and left me feeling ashamed.

Letting go of perfectionism, accepting that things can be really good without being perfect, has been ongoing work in my recovery. I've learned to see things as they are and not through the distorting lens of depression. Whereas depression makes all negatives huge and all positives tiny (if you can see them at all), reality works to give everything its proper size. You don't deny or avoid the negative; you just don't supersize it.

Finally, one doesn't need to do this alone. My ability now to enjoy my memories of Flashlight's funeral is the result of the conversation I had with the little boy's parents. By telling them how bad I felt, I learned that my ignorance about Flashlight was universally shared by those who knew and loved her/him. As so often has been true in my recovery, opening up to the appropriate person, not letting shame keep me isolated, transformed everything. These days, I remember that service from long ago, and I say to myself, "Job well done."

Help 12

Losing Control and Finding Hope

Emily Dickinson wrote,

> "Hope" is the thing with feathers—
> That perches in the soul—[15]

This is a rich image of hope, one capable of many interpretations. I'm drawn to the verb *perches*, to the image of hope being free to perch where it will. Since I believe there is no recovery without hope, it is hard for me to accept that this essential element is not in my control. I rely on it to get up in the morning and to fall asleep at night. When things are going badly, I need hope to sustain me on the journey and not to let depression pull me under. So much depends upon hope, yet like a skittish bird, it perches where it will.

In my recovery, I have sought to let go of control and to open my life fully to hope. For so long, attempting to control situations and people has been my way of coping with anxiety, an attempt to keep my life walled off from anything that might cause distress. I look back and see my need to control poisoning every area of my life, from keeping a stranglehold on the family finances to trying to manage every detail at church. The latter was brought home by a former parishioner. "Bob," she said, "you were a good minister in so many ways, even if you could be a little bit controlling from time to time." I didn't really want to hear that, but I know now that, as gently as she could, she was telling me the truth.

Over many years of ministry, I had come to take more and more responsibility for the church on myself, increasingly doing the work and making the decisions that belonged to others. I sought to control how people thought of me, trying to anticipate what people wanted and then trying to make it happen before they asked. Likewise, I'd try to anticipate what people didn't want and to make sure that never happened. I'd be the perfect minister, and people would have no choice but to like me.

What I was doing had nothing to do with enjoying power or taking pleasure in dominating other people. Far from it. I felt like a slave, forever seeking to respond to every parishioner's wishes. Always hypervigilant, I exhausted myself trying to keep everything calm and everybody happy. In this way, I could forestall anxiety and live in peace, except that anxiety permeated everything that I was doing.

I'm quick to say that this had little to do with reality, little to do with my parishioners being more demanding or critical than the norm. On balance, trying to be honest about the joy and pain of working with people in all their complexity, I believe that I was fortunate in the congregations I served. My need to control wasn't about them; it was about me—my anxiety and my depression.

Trying to meet every demand, including the unspoken ones, is exhausting. Ultimately fatigue and despair overwhelmed me. If my image of hope is a bird perching wherever it wills, then my image of control is a juggler struggling to keep too many balls in the air. I think back on myself as having more and more balls tossed at me to juggle, more and more demands I had to anticipate and meet to keep my control intact. Finally, I just couldn't do it any more—one ball fell, then two, finally all of them. The collapse led me to the emergency room and then to the psych unit. When I looked around, there were dropped balls lying all over the floor.

On the locked unit, I was stripped of the capacity to control much of anything. I did what I was told as well as I could. One would think this total and very public loss of control was the worst thing that could possibly happen to someone like me. In many ways it was just that, but now I also see it as a moment of liberation. I was in the hospital, true, but I wasn't dead and I didn't have to juggle anymore. Thank God.

Over time I moved back into the world of activity and responsibility, the world where there is juggling to be done. I learned to be careful to pick up only the balls that belonged to me and to leave other balls lying on the floor for somebody else to pick up. With each of my important relationships, I've needed to work through issues of control, what part is mine and what part is somebody else's. When I returned to my profession, I worked to establish healthy boundaries in my relationships and not repeat the past pattern of trying to control other people. In my anxiety, I can still pick up responsibilities that aren't mine, but I know my tendencies and I'm learning how to back off.

These are vital learnings, yet my ability to give up trying to control is grounded in something deeper. I can't say there is a logical path from control to hope. I simply know that in my recovery hope has done much to free me from my need to control by offering me a better way of coping with anxiety. If control is about fear of the future, then hope is about being open to the future. Control, living to prevent bad things from happening, is exhausting. Hope, living in the possibility that good things might happen, is not exhausting at all.

This is why Dickinson's image of hope is so powerful for me. Hope perches where it will; there is no controlling it. That said, and said emphatically, it doesn't mean that I must wait passively for hope to come my way. For example, I am a casual birder at best, but I do know enough to pick the right seeds to make it more likely that colorful birds will perch on my feeder. Ultimately they come or they don't, but I can do my part to make it more likely that they will. When they do, it's wonderful. One memorable morning, I looked out and saw two indigo buntings perched on our feeder. Years later, I still get a thrill when I remember seeing them.

I have also learned there are things I can do to make it more likely that hope will come to me. I can hang out with people who make me feel more hopeful when I am around them. I encourage you to stay close to people who are bringers of hope in your own life. Sometimes all one needs to do is remember good times in the past, and hope will come. In its many forms, worship can be a time for hope to come. If you have a faith tradition, I encourage you to seek its words and images of hope and then draw as close to them as you can.

In the last stanza of Emily Dickinson's poem, we are assured that this thing with feathers can come to us no matter where we are, even in the most difficult situations, even in really bad times when we feel unable to do anything to invite it in. The speaker tells us that hope is always possible because, in the end, it is beyond our control and it demands nothing of us.

> I've heard it in the chilliest land—
> And on the strangest Sea—
> Yet—never—in Extremity,
> It asked a crumb—of me.[16]

Help 13

Finding a Safe Place

EVERY MORNING MY ALARM clock goes off, and I wake up to a miracle. Someone watching through the window (actually, someone watching through the window would feel creepy) would see only the least miraculous and the most ordinary: me opening my eyes, then fumbling around to turn off the alarm clock, maybe uttering an appropriate expletive if I see that it snowed overnight, and finally getting up out of bed.

That's the miracle: getting out of bed. Granted it's not the parting-of-the-Red-Sea kind of miracle, but if it's a miracle to do what was once impossible, then chalk one up. If restful sleep or getting out of bed without a struggle sounds impossible to you right now, then I invite you to believe in miracles.

For so long, this miracle didn't happen. In the depths of my depression, I'd lie in bed with a pillow over my head. I'd hear the alarm clock and I would despair, knowing that the longer I stayed in bed the worse the rest of the day was going to be. I'd press the pillow down on my face as hard as I could, blotting out all sound and sight. Finally my wife's pleas or the urgency of something I could not avoid would force me out of bed.

Hiding in bed, I had no energy to face the world and its demands. I felt adequate for nothing and desperately needed a safe place. Under my pillow with the door closed, nothing could get at me. Though I couldn't stop the scenarios of self-judgment and self-hatred running in my mind, I could avoid some new failure, some further cause for self-contempt. I could also avoid the stress of trying to act normal when I couldn't play the part.

Hiding in bed kept me safe from the outside world, but I couldn't stay there. The psych unit was also a safe place, but it cost my freedom. For a time I was quite willing to pay that cost. I couldn't get out of the locked doors, but trouble couldn't get in—more than a fair enough trade off as far as I was concerned.

Maybe this search for a safe place goes back to when we were children. Our parents, if we were fortunate to have healthy and loving parents, were the sanctuary from which we could venture forth into the world. We felt safe to go out because we knew that, if the world got too much for us, we could hurry home to safety. Over time we developed more confidence in venturing further from home, but we could always go back to our safe place when we needed to.

In recovery I've learned that family is still a safe place for many of us. This is how it is for me: my wife and my adult children are my safest of safe places. I know others who've created a family of close friends they can count on to be trustworthy and understanding. For others it is a group that will be there for them no matter what happens: maybe the community where they worship, maybe their AA group or some recovery community like Vail Place, maybe friends they've bonded with over the years for whatever reason. There are many groups that can provide safe places. If we have more than one such family or group in our lives, if we have multiple safe places, then we are blessed.

Given how important it is to connect with other people during recovery, it is natural that families and communities become safe places. I also know how helpful a safe physical place can be in recovery; sometimes it is essential. Some people turn their rooms into sanctuaries, decorated with objects that are talismans of safety and security. Pictures of loved ones, those we have felt safe with in the past, can transform a room into a safe place. For many, a pet brings affection and joy into an otherwise ordinary space. After a day out in the world, simply coming home and entering one's safe place melts the stress away. Tragically for homeless people living with a mental illness, the lack of such a safe physical place makes recovery all the more difficult.

For each of us, there are personal choices we make about what to include in order to transform a physical space into a safe place. There are also choices we make about what to leave out. In my physical safe place, the room where I'm writing this book, I don't want to have a clock visible. If I did, I'd be watching it, constantly looking up at it judging how much I've gotten done. The clock would turn into a stressor. I don't want a radio dialed into the news. Again, a stressor. I don't want diplomas on the walls.

On bad days, diplomas stand for promises unfulfilled. I invite you to edit your safe place, removing anything that doesn't help.

In *Breakfast at Tiffany's*, Holly Golightly (Audrey Hepburn) has found her safe place at Tiffany's, the elegant jewelry store: "Calms me down right away, the quietness and proud look of it, nothing very bad could happen to you there."[17] This is a clinically precise definition of what a safe place feels like. Holly teaches us that safe places are wherever we find them—maybe our home, but maybe a store like Tiffany's, a museum or theater, a restaurant, a coffee shop, a bar, a park, or a ballpark—wherever you feel safe and calm. In serving churches, I've known people who just come by, not at a scheduled time of worship or for a program, to sit quietly in the sanctuary, to be still and at peace, to find calm and a momentary respite from the world and its demands. I hope they found what they sought.

With the safe places I have found in my own life, I no longer need to turn my bed into one. My morning miracle is now a routine; safe places do this for us. Whatever it is, time in a safe place renews and restores so we can face life with deeper emotional resources, more at peace and less on edge. Sitting in a comfortable chair in your room, maybe with your dog curled at your feet, or a good friend sitting across from you—wherever it is—when you feel the way Holly describes, you'll know that you've found your safe place.

Help 14

Honoring Your Story

AFTER MORE THAN A year of not working following my second hospitalization, I had my first job interview. The possible job had a clear beginning and end. I would serve three months, covering for another minister who was going on a sabbatical leave. My therapist, psychiatrist, wife, and I had agreed that this short-term position would be a safe test to determine whether I could go back to work full-time. With their support, as well as the effectiveness of the medications I was on, I felt pretty sure I could do three months. I could see the finish line before I started the race.

I made sure I was on time to the interview. Actually I was there twenty minutes early, so I sat in my car looking at my watch. I checked several times in the rearview mirror to make sure my tie was centered and there were no coffee stains at the corners of my mouth. A couple of minutes before the appointment time, I got out of my car and walked to the most likely of the church doors. It was unlocked, and there was someone waiting inside to welcome me.

The five members of the interview team were dressed casually. I had on a jacket and that well-centered necktie pulled up tight to my collar. It was the first time I'd dressed up since before I was hospitalized. We sat in a circle around a table in the church social hall. The chairs were old and comfortable, and the rest of the furnishings were a classic church mix of donations and the best items from previous rummage sales.

Whatever I had expected or feared, the five people on the search committee did their best to make me feel at home—no inquisition, no good cop/bad cop interrogation. Still, as soon as I started talking, I could feel my throat getting tighter and my hands and stomach starting to clench. Could they notice that my voice sounded odd?

Their questions were fair and appropriate; I had anticipated most of them. They had sent me information about the church and a job description. I had read the material over and over, memorizing lots of facts, just like I used to do for a history test in high school. I'm sure I answered a little stiffly, talked too rapidly, and tried too hard to make sure they knew how much I'd studied for the interview, but overall I think I handled their questions well enough.

It's what they didn't ask that threw me: why had I left the church I'd served so long and what had happened during the year-plus gap in my résumé? I'd assumed they would ask, and I'd rehearsed answers over and over in my mind. When they didn't raise the issue and my turn came to ask questions, I felt I had to be forthcoming. I laid it all out, saying something like, "You know I haven't worked for some time because I'm suffering from major depression. It's a serious mental illness. I was hospitalized twice for it, and now I'm on medication and seeing a therapist. My therapist and I agree that I'm doing a lot better and that it's safe for me to apply for this job."

The more I talked about my illness, the tighter my throat got. I started to sweat. Maybe it was my imagination, but I think the members of the committee physically recoiled a little. The interview ended soon after that, and the chair of the committee said she'd get back to me ASAP. When she called me, she said that though it had been a hard choice and though they felt I was a great candidate, they'd decided to go with somebody else. I didn't ask her why; I thought I knew.

I went into a mini-tailspin after what felt like a personal rejection, a major hit for my self-esteem. Wisely I made a special appointment with my therapist to tell him what had happened. He helped me calm down and not take the loss so personally. He reassured me that one turndown hardly meant I wouldn't be able to find a job in the future. Then he put his hand on my shoulder and said, "Bob, I respect your honesty and, of course, there's no shame about mental illness. You know how much we've talked about that. But you get to decide when you tell your story and who you tell it to. I don't think a job interview is the place to volunteer that information."

His words have meant a lot to me in my recovery: I get to decide. He was telling me that I'm an agent and that I have freedom and control over my story, as well as control over many other aspects of my life. Being able to decide is part of my dignity as a human being. It nurtures my self-respect. My story cost me a lot, a price I'm still paying. If I put it out there, I want to do it because I choose to.

For all of us, whatever our mental illness story is, it cost us a lot. We need to pause and let the implications of that cost sink in. The jazz saxophonist Charlie Parker is said to have put it this way, "If you don't live it, it won't come out of your horn." For Parker, who knew so much pain in his own life, it was the cost of the power of his music, the price he paid for the truth to come out of his horn. Like him we pay a high cost in pain for our stories. Our stories are precious, and we are the only ones who get to decide when we tell them, how we tell them, and who we tell them to.

That said, there are important reasons to tell our stories. They have power to push back stigma and to quiet those who would shame us. I started telling my story to other patients while I was in the hospital. Now I tell it more formally, often to a group of strangers who are interested in a mental health topic. I tell them the truth about my illness and my recovery. My story commands their full attention.

I so much hope that people hearing my story will have a show-and-tell experience. Because I am to able tell my story and tell it well—I give myself the credit I've earned—I show that recovery is possible. After I'm done, people often pull me aside and tell me their personal mental illness stories. When this happens, I am so grateful that I chose to tell mine.

If someone had told me early in my recovery that I would one day be doing these talks, I would have been tempted to ask whether they thought I would be telling my story before or after I won my Olympic gold medal for pole vaulting. In other words, it was never going to happen. But it has, and I don't intend for it to stop.

As you can tell, doing these talks means a lot to me. But even after doing this so many times, I still take my time before agreeing to do another talk. I honor my freedom to decide, and I honor my story. I'm giving these talks because I've chosen to. If for some reason it doesn't feel like a free choice, I'll turn down the invitation.

I think back to that first job interview, and now I can smile. I have to wonder what those good folks on the search committee thought when I told them my story. I suspect that they felt like they'd gotten way more than they bargained for. I give myself credit for being honest and telling the truth about myself. I won't put myself down for doing what felt like the right thing at the time. It's just that I've moved on in my recovery. I feel in control of my story, and I intend never to forget the price I paid for telling it. There's an old Bible verse that tells us there's a time to keep silence and a time to speak. That's exactly what I'm trying to say, and I get to decide what time it is.

Help 15

Finding Community, Dignity, and Agency

Vail Place Uptown, a big old house in south Minneapolis, is a clubhouse for people living with mental illness. Instead of staying home alone, watching TV, and snacking on processed food, you can go to Vail Place, read the paper, hang out with friends, sign up for a movie or some other form of social recreation, have a nutritious meal at a minimal price, and generally enjoy life as a valued member of a community. There are more than 290 such clubhouses around the world, including our sister clubhouse in Hopkins, a western suburb of Minneapolis.

In addition to being a clubhouse, Vail Place is also a social service agency, a one-stop shop for people living with mental illness. The staff helps people deal with issues of housing, education, employment, access to physical and mental health services, as well as access to the myriad of government programs they might be eligible for.

Every morning at half past nine and every afternoon at one o'clock, we have two "work ordered day" meetings. At the downstairs meeting (which I attend), we divvy up the jobs that need to be done to maintain the clubhouse and to provide meals: vacuuming and cleaning, maintenance, staffing and stocking the snack bar, taking out the trash and recyclables, managing the lunch sign-up, and helping with the raft of kitchen jobs needed to provide a nutritious hot meal for thirty people or so. At the upstairs meeting, members volunteer to do another set of tasks to sustain the clubhouse: writing the newsletter, maintaining records, enrolling new members, developing programs, working on fund-raisers, maintaining a small bank for members, and doing other tasks that are part of the life of a small nonprofit.

The culture of Vail Place is open and easy, with members always free not to volunteer for a job at one of these meetings. That's OK—you've already accomplished a lot by coming to the clubhouse. It's great that you are here. But some of the jobs are very easy, and you have the daily encouragement of other people volunteering. It turns out that over time most people volunteer for a job: "I can dust." "I can wash dishes." "I'll stock the snack bar if you show me where the supplies are." "Show me how, and I'll roll the silverware." "I did data entry in my old job." "I'm actually good at filling out forms." Often somebody who's volunteered for a job asks a new member to help, making it easy to enter into the world of contributing to the life of their clubhouse.

One thing about these meetings has intrigued me ever since I started going to Vail Place. You can attend meeting after meeting and watch the tasks being distributed, but you won't be able to figure out who's a clubhouse member, who's staff, and who's a volunteer. To be totally honest, if you go long enough, you might see a trend: staff and volunteers wait a beat or two as people volunteer for jobs to make sure they don't take a job that a member wants to do.

This is by design: the goal is to have members manage their clubhouse as much as possible. At Vail Place people living with mental illness are not patients; rather, they are members who have a stake in the future of their clubhouse. There are regular decision-making meetings where members and staff meet together to make the decisions necessary to run the facility. This process extends to hiring new staff. Members have huge input in the interviewing and selection process. Member involvement, member input, member governance of their own clubhouse—it's the day-to-day practice of Vail Place.

This practice expresses an understanding that recovery from mental illness includes the recovery of agency. By "agency" I mean the freedom to choose. I have described how my therapist helped me understand that because I am an agent, I am free to decide whether to tell my mental illness story. At Vail Place, I've learned the full power of agency to give one's life dignity and value.

Mental illness creates fear and destroys self-confidence, so decisions are terribly hard to make. At a very low point in my depression, I panicked trying to decide what to order at Bunny's, a restaurant that I'd been to countless times before. I knew much of the menu by heart—comfort food and old favorites—but on this day I just could not decide what to order. I felt like everybody in the restaurant was staring at me, and if I didn't make a choice, they'd start laughing at me. The pressure was too great. When the server came to take my order, I could not put words together. My wife, seeing my panic, ordered a burger and fries for me.

When mental illness leads to hospitalization, then even the possibility of making decisions, of being in charge of one's own life, is taken away. You don't get to decide about much of anything beyond the limited options you have for breakfast, lunch, and dinner. If your mental illness has brought you into the legal system, again there is a huge loss of agency. Even if you are at home, the arena in which you are free to make your own decisions has been circumscribed: maybe you're not working, maybe you're not driving, maybe you're just not going out of the house much. In ways large and small, mental illness reduces one's freedom of choice.

Vail Place counters this loss by encouraging agency whenever possible. This process begins with a member's decision to come on a particular day. The invitation and welcome are always there, but the member decides whether to come. At the clubhouse, the member decides whether to take a job and make a contribution. If it's a decision-making meeting day, the member can experience having an impact on the life of the community. When a therapist tells you that your life makes a difference, you hope it's true. At Vail Place you experience your life making a difference, and you know it's true.

For some members, this strengthening of agency extends beyond the walls of the clubhouse. Vail Place has an employment program that enables members to transition from voluntary jobs in-house to paid work at various businesses and institutions in the community. Of course, added responsibility and demands can make this a stressful time. Staff support these members and work with employers, doing all they can to make the transition successful. It's a challenge, but the payoff in terms of increased self-respect and self-confidence makes the challenge worthwhile.

Some members of Vail Place never go on to work outside the clubhouse. Mental illness, physical disability, age, the lack of available jobs—there are many reasons why a member might not transition to employment. Not to worry, Vail Place continues to provide community, offer activities, and nourish agency. Wherever a person is in recovery, Vail Place can help.

As I seek to do for myself, I encourage you to find places in your life where your freedom to make decisions is encouraged and strengthened. I also encourage you to check out the website for Clubhouse International, www.clubhouse-intl.org, to see whether there is a clubhouse close to you. If there is, I urge you to call, arrange a visit, and consider becoming a member. The process is easy, it's free, and the benefits can be enormous.

Help 16

Finding the Truth

I WASN'T LOOKING FOR a revelation. I was just in a hurry to mail a package, but things weren't going well. As soon as I turned into the parking lot of my local post office, I could see that I'd picked a bad time to go there. Why was the parking lot almost packed when we weren't close to any holiday? I was sure I'd have to wait in line. Well, at least I could get a move on so nobody could get in line in front of me. I took one of the few remaining parking places, grabbed my package, and got out of the car as quickly as I could. With rapid steps, I headed toward the post office door, determined that the next place in line was mine.

Not so fast! In my peripheral vision, I saw a woman about my age heading toward the same destination. Like me, her jaw was set and her pace was rapid. No question about it, we both wanted that next place in line. A quick calibration of our combined velocities and angles of approach indicated that we would arrive at the door of the post office simultaneously, making a collision inevitable. As the door drew closer, we both surreptitiously sped up, still short of all-out running, but we were both rapidly getting there. Clearly, a lot was at stake for both of us.

To avoid the fast-approaching collision, some mutual acknowledgement of each other's presence became necessary. Maybe if I stuck out my arms and wiggled them up and down like a jet fighter trying to avoid colliding with a hostile aircraft, she'd back off. But before I could get my arms extended, she looked over at me, smiled, and asked, "Wanna race?" I burst out laughing and so did she. What else were we going to do?

We slowed down and walked in side by side. There are two doors to the post office. I held the first one for her, and she held the second for me.

We stood in line together, shared some small talk, and waited for our turns. Fittingly, when we arrived at the front of the line, two clerks were available, so we both mailed our packages at the same time. The race to get our packages in the mail had ended in a tie.

The revelation in this story isn't that I can be impatient to the point of near rudeness. I know that, and I'm working on it as part of my effort to simply calm down and keep things in perspective. The revelation isn't that even in trivial things I can be far more competitive than I'd like to admit. Again, I own it, and I'm working on it. No, the revelation came with her question, "Wanna race?" She popped the bubble by naming what we were both thinking and doing, the elephant in the post office parking lot, the honest-to-God truth about what was going on.

For those of us in recovery from mental illness, revelations can happen anywhere, from the post office parking lot to the office of our therapist. Some years ago my therapist wrote a few words on a piece of paper and then handed it to me. He had written, "My father doesn't get to decide for me anymore." At that time I was in my late fifties, and my father had been dead for many years. Those facts didn't matter. Like the woman in the post office parking lot, my therapist had absolutely nailed the truth of the situation. I was still trying to please my father, trying to gain approval that would never come. I've needed to read that piece of paper over and over for this basic truth to change me. God bless my dad, but I'm doing my best now to live my own life and to make my decisions on the basis of what would be best for the people I love and the things I care about.

Revelations that cut to the truth of life can indeed happen anywhere. Maybe something doesn't qualify as a full-blown revelation, but it can still contain needed wisdom. For example, Gilda Radner famously said, "I base my fashion taste on what doesn't itch." Me too. Once I was in the ROTC program at a southern high school, where I wore a long-sleeved woolen shirt when the temperature was in the nineties and the humidity was punishing. Forever after, I have based my fashion sense on what doesn't itch. I never admitted it like Gilda Radner, but it's what I do, and I'm admitting it now. The more I think about her straightforwardness, common sense, and honesty, as well as her unwillingness to let others force her to itch, the more I believe that her fashion sense is, in fact, a revelation in full.

One of my most important revelations came many years ago. I was meeting with the youth group at the first church that I served. The kids were asking me questions about being a minister, everything from did I really believe in God and the Bible to whether it was ever right to tell a lie and to how much I got paid. I tried to be honest and respectful to their questions, but I'm afraid sometimes I got pretty abstract and too theological. When I answered the question about my salary honestly, I could tell that, in their minds, they were comparing it not to what their folks were making but to their own allowances. Compared to what they were taking in, I was rich. No way was I going to get any sympathy from them.

When it was almost time for the session to end, one of the girls looked at me and said, "You're a good minister because you care about people." For her this was the truth, as obvious and straightforward as "Wanna race?" from that woman in the parking lot. She gave me a gift, the truth as she saw it, a few words that I hold close to my heart. Yes, I have been controlling, and I own up to some serious errors in my work, but I really do care about people. In times when I have professional doubts and questions, when depression was trashing it all, I think about what that girl said, and I smile.

HELP 17

Finding Meaning

In *A CATSKILL EAGLE*, a murder mystery by Robert Parker, at a critical moment Detective Spenser tells his friend Hawk, "I am trying to make sense out of stuff I don't understand." And Hawk responds, "That's called life, babe."[18]

There are definitions of life that are more philosophically sophisticated than Spenser's, but on any given day, his definition pretty much nails it. In my recovery, I'm doing what the detective describes: trying to make sense out of stuff I don't understand. Why did my life take such a terrible detour? What does it mean? How can I make sure that it doesn't happen again? Can I redeem what has happened to me by using it to help others? Answering these and similar questions has occupied much of my time in recovery.

Sometimes I ask myself whether this is really the best use of my time. Maybe it would be better to stop rummaging around in the past, revisiting old hurts. Maybe it would be better to leave the past behind, get on with my life, and let the meaning unfold as it may. The truth is that I can't, and I don't think any of us can. Like the moment when we start feeling hungry or thirsty, the questions about meaning come without any conscious deciding on our part. They're not in our control, and we can't get rid of them. There's simply something about us that craves an explanation, and it won't go away. It's how we're put together and what makes us tick; it's what's called life, babe.

I believe our innate need to seek meaning can be an ally for us in recovery. The key is to not push too hard or demand too much. I've learned to settle for partial understandings and to accept that I'll never finish the puzzle. For example, there is a critical event in my story that I do not fully understand: I called my wife at the moment when suicidal thoughts came so very close to overwhelming me. I'd had these thoughts before and had not picked up the phone. This time I did. Why? If I said I knew the answer, that would be a lie. I've gone over the event so many times in therapy, and something about it always slips past me. *Grace* is the best word I have for what happened.

Still, as time has passed, some things have become clearer to me. Now I realize that I was fortunate to have had someone to call. Many people living with mental illness are isolated and feel no one is there to pick up the phone. (However, I'm quick to add, there is always someone you can call. Call 911. Call the Suicide Prevention Hotline 1–800–273–8255. There are people who want to help right now if you need them.) Also, though my depression had done damage to our marriage, I knew my wife still loved me, as did our two adult children. At that moment I could not bring myself to hurt them by hurting myself.

Trying to make sense of that phone call has caused me to focus my full attention on the enormous resource that the love of my family is for me in recovery. It has been always there, but I've taken it for granted. Realizing their support is vital for me in recovery. I intend never to take it for granted again.

It has also been worth it to wrestle with other questions that are part of my story. Why did I demand so much of myself? Why was I so afraid of up-setting other people? Why did I turn everything into some kind of demand? Why am I so quick to blame myself and so slow to forgive? I don't have a com-plete answer to any of these questions, but trying to answer them has done much to enhance my recovery. Over time I've learned much more about how my behavior fits into patterns. Understanding myself, even incompletely, has made me less anxious and has given me a greater sense of control over my life. I know much more about what triggers my depression, what to watch out for, and—for this I am very grateful—what makes me happy.

Help in understanding these behavioral patterns has come from many places. Therapy has been essential, as has learning more about my illness from books and online. For example, the first time I read *Feeling Good* by David Burns, I felt a major piece of my life's puzzle snap into place. He offers a vivid description of *personalization,* a cognitive distortion that he terms "the mother of guilt."[19] It's not as if the word *personalization* was new to me or as if it hadn't ever occurred to me that I take things too personally. But how frequently I personalize, how I do it without thinking, how it's at the center of a pattern—these ideas were new to me.

Burns writes about personalization, "You arbitrarily conclude that what happened was your fault or reflects your inadequacy, even when you were not responsible for it."[20] This could be a sentence taken from an objective analysis of my first thirty years as a pastor. A roof leak, a lost coffee pot, a poorly attended service, a decline in income—it was all my fault, and I never forgot to punish myself for it. Learning about this behavioral pattern, bringing it into the light, was my first step in changing my behavior.

One would expect to find help in self-understanding from a therapist or a book on mood therapy. And so I have, but I've also found help from more unusual places. I keep coming back to what I learned from people on the psych unit. Remember the elderly woman who shared her Styrofoam bowl of mixed nuts with me? She said, "I took pleasure for granted. That was my big mistake. Take your eye off pleasure, and you will lose it." Her words capture a major theme in my recovery, and I'll let them stand here for all that I have learned from people living with mental illness.

I encourage you to stay vigilant, watching for help and understanding from unexpected places. I've learned about myself from movies, from books that had nothing to do with mood therapy or mental illness, and from a woman in the parking lot at the post office. I've learned from Elvis, poets, walks in the park, free-range money, snake handling, drumming, a late guinea pig, Gilda Radner, and Robert Parker. And more than half the book is still to come! Just as we can't control when questions about our life's meaning might arise, we also can't control where an answer might come. Recovery is pain and struggle; it's also these moments when answers come and pieces snap into place. It's times when we feel the thing with feathers perch on our shoulder.

From sources both obvious and emphatically not obvious, I have learned about my life and my mental illness. In responding to my human craving to make sense of things, I have learned about my patterns of behavior and the changes I need to make to be happy and at peace in the world. For all of us, recovery moves along as we make more sense of behaviors that we do not fully understand. It's what's called life, babe.

HELP 18

Becoming Slow to Judge

WHILE SERVING AS A parish minister, I tried to visit each of our home-bound members at least once a month. Some visits were sad, some routine, and some wonderful. Visiting Dorcas, a little woman in her early nineties, topped the list of the wonderful visits.

Dorcas—funny, great at telling stories, able to look life in the eye—made visiting a pleasure. She always let me know she was pleased I had come. She would start the visit by asking me questions about church that I was glad to answer. Without being too obvious, she always found a way to let me know that she thought I was doing a good job. When I was with her, I loved being a minister.

Like me, she was a great fan of our Minnesota Twins baseball team. She listened to every game on the radio and kept score on her homemade scorecards. A tall stack of them sat on the card table beside her easy chair, next to a coffee cup full of well-sharpened pencils. When we talked base-ball, she knew what she was talking about, and she loved to talk baseball.

She also loved to bake. She could have been a pastry chef in another life. On most visits, as I opened the door, I was drawn into her small apart-ment by the aroma of cookies baking. As soon as I walked in, she'd put cookies on the table—she didn't even make me wait—and she'd start to make coffee. While we waited for the coffee, she encouraged me to try one of her freshly baked chocolate-chip cookies as a pre-coffee appetizer. Who was I to turn her down?

Then, and I guess it was inevitable, there was a visit that didn't go so well. After the coffee had percolated—she made it old-school—she put the pot in the sink. Did she think we'd already had our coffee and now it was time to clean up? Or was she having a black-out moment when time and place fell away from her? So sad, I didn't want to accept that time catches up with us all, even Dorcas. Well, she'd had a great run anyway. Soon Dorcas, or more likely one of her daughters, would have to find a facility where she could be safe and well looked after.

She read the pitying look on my face, laughed, and said, "I know this looks weird, but I'm too weak some days to hold up the coffeepot and fill the cups. So I set the pot in the sink, and then I can tip it enough to fill them. If some spills—who cares?—it's already in the sink. When you get to be my age, you have to learn how to compensate for what you can't do."

Without spilling a drop, she carried the two filled coffee cups to the table. "Here, have another cookie. I love having somebody to bake for." I did, and I did again after that. As we ate together, she told me that the problem with the Twins current first baseman was that he had let himself get too darn fat. Good guy, good player, but he did seem to be carrying a lot of pizza under his belt, making it hard for him to bend down for those low throws. For Dorcas he could have been a grandson who needed to go on a diet.

The Twins have played a lot of games since I last visited with Dorcas— they've won some and lost more. But there's always next year! Even now there are times when something happens in a Twins game or an announcer mentions that long-retired first baseman's name, and then I remember Dorcas and how much I appreciated her kindness and hospitality. Even more than that, I am grateful because she taught me an important recovery lesson. Watching her with the coffeepot in the sink, I had made a judgment about her, made it without thinking, and I couldn't have been more wrong. Far from losing it, Dorcas had figured it out. Can't hold the coffeepot? No problem, set it in the sink. Fortunately, though it was clear that she knew what I was thinking, she was able to laugh it off. No harm done.

I don't always get off so easy. Sometimes I've acted on my judgments about other people, on their supposed motives and desires, and then later learned I had completely misunderstood the situation. I've done even worse to myself. I've judged myself cruelly, beaten up on myself both mentally and physically. Since I didn't have enough time to finish beating up on myself in the daytime, I'd keep going at night, lying awake, cold and sweaty, reviewing in vivid detail all my sins and failures. In the weeks before my hospitalizations, my self-judgments got sharper and hit harder. No excuses, no mitigating circumstances—I am a rotten failure. My self-judgments came close to killing me. In recovery I've learned to cut a lot more slack for myself and for other people. I agree with the sentiment that most people, most of the time, are doing the best they can. Maybe there is a time for judgment—as we know, there truly are some bad actors out there—but not before trying to understand and giving other people the benefit of the doubt.

In her novel *Gilead*, Marilynne Robinson writes about a character, "The waters never parted for him, not once in his life, so far as I know."[21] This brings to mind people I've known for whom things just never seemed to go right, no matter what they did or how hard they tried. They could never catch a break; the waters never parted for them. They need my compassion, not my judgment. At times, I have felt like one of them.

I am working hard in recovery to do for myself as I am learning to do for others. There are still times when I feel a flash of shame, when I want to hit myself for something I said or did. But there is much less of this now. Most days I can accept that (like other people) I am doing the best that I can, and (like them) I need compassion not judgment. I've learned that judging myself stops me in my tracks, making change and growth impossible. That is the antithesis of recovery.

I'm not done absorbing these lessons, but I'm making progress, enough to deserve a reward. In my mind, I'm off to visit Dorcas, have a couple of chocolate-chip cookies, and share her concern that our beloved first baseman has packed on yet a couple more pounds.

Help 19

Escaping Self-Accusative Thoughts

I'VE HEARD THEM CALLED many things: "self-accusative thoughts," "obsessive thoughts," "racing thoughts," "intrusive thoughts," and "ruminations." They are the swarming thoughts that never leave your mind at peace. Sometimes they're just loud enough to make sure you know they're there. Sometimes they turn up the volume so high they're the only thing there.

My self-accusative thoughts have perfect memories. They can recall all my mistakes, both great and small, keeping each mistake fresh and lively. They have a gift for telling me exactly what will make me feel most ashamed and most worthless at any given moment. And in case I missed it, they tell me over and over again.

These thoughts are like swarming insects, and Minnesotans know a lot about noxious insects. We have the Boundary Waters Canoe Area (BWCA), a paradise with dappled lakes and singing breezes. Here the days soften into night, the stars slowly open their eyes, and the last smile of sunlight drifts off to sleep. All this while the baby waves lap gently against the cuddling sand. And here too, as sweet night opens wide her embrace, there's a sudden God-awful racket as countless insects—mosquitoes, black flies, buzzing whatevers—seize the night, fly up your nose, and feast on all your body parts.

Like a hunted animal, you race for safety, diving into your tent and searching for whatever insect repellant you can get your hands on. You spray and spray. When you're well lathered, you head back outside to the campfire, hoping the smoke will be added help in repelling your tormentors. Soon you're standing so close to the fire your shoes start to smoke. It's another night in the BWCA.

The mosquitoes, black flies, and buzzing whatevers—these are dead ringers for self-accusative thoughts. Like noxious insects, these thoughts spoil everything, so you're frantically looking for any way to escape them. Over time I've learned that some accusative thoughts are defeated by medication and others succumb to individual therapy; some are zapped by cognitive behavioral therapy, and others are done in by telling my story to people I trust.

So it goes until there aren't many self-accusative thoughts buzzing around in my head anymore. Still, for a fuller recovery and more joy in life, I need to find a way to deal with the ones that are left. I think again of my times in the BWCA. The truth is that unless it's so cold that you don't want to be there anyway, there will always be insects when you go camping. There's no way to totally escape them. You can use all the best insect repellant you have and stand by the fire until you're well done, but the insects will still be a nuisance. Granted, a nuisance is a lot better than a plague, but still it's a nuisance. Isn't there some way to make them all just go away?

But hold on a minute. There's an obvious question that should have been asked first: why would you go out into such torment? Why not just stay in your tent, wrapped up like a mummy, and go to sleep? (Well, try to sleep anyway. The rocks and roots don't make a good mattress, but that's another story.) You stay outside your tent at night because it is the BWCA, where on a clear night the Milky Way arches across the sky, where the moon makes shadows, and where there's always a chance—not most nights, but just maybe—that you will be given the gift of the northern lights. In the BWCA I've watched them twice at once: sitting in a canoe on a lake with a friend, I looked up and saw the northern lights in the sky, and then I looked down and saw them in the water. Have that experience once and you'll always try to have it again. Insects can't compete with the northern lights.

Just as there is much in the BWCA that can make you forget about insects, so there are many things in our recovery that can help us forget about our remaining self-accusative thoughts. And thankfully, these things are close at hand, not like a rare display of the northern lights. For example, even when I was in the hospital and obsessive thoughts were buzzing loudly, I had conversations with other patients that took me so totally out of myself that I didn't hear those self-accusative thoughts. For a blessed time, I was not in my own head, but rather I was fully engaged with another person. Since then I have had more and more conversations that have taken me out of myself, and my recovery has thrived.

I've mentioned how my friend can become so at one with his drumming that there is no opening for mental illness and how writing does the same for me. For athletes, there is "the zone" where they are totally absorbed in their sports. Artists say they can get lost for hours in their work, thinking of nothing but what they are creating. The same is true for people who get caught up cheering for their favorite team, concentrating on fine handwork, practicing yoga, cooking a gourmet meal, planning a trip, binging on a favorite TV series, working out, watching their cat, or doing any of the multitude of things that allows them to get lost in something outside their own minds.

As I look back to the time when depression dominated my life, self-accusative thoughts (often manifested in scenarios replete with failure and shame) made my life unbearable. Other symptoms were awful, but self-accusative thoughts were the symptom I could not abide. My own mind had turned against me, and I had no place where I could go and just be still. Now I count as a treasure anything that absorbs my attention and silences these tormentors. I am grateful for the treasures I've already found, and I am always looking for more.

Help 20

Learning to Not Beat Up on Yourself

SELF-DISGUST, SELF-ANGER, SELF-HARM—MY DEPRESSION turned me into my own unforgiving enemy. In black and white during the day and in Technicolor at night, the endless catalogue of my mistakes and failures played on the movie screen of my mind, and all the exits from my mental theater were blocked. In recovery I've found some kinder ways of understanding my life that have helped me become more self-accepting.

THE FIRST STONE

In a beloved Bible story, found in John's gospel, Jesus stands with a woman who was caught in adultery. The legal authorities bring her before Jesus and tell him that the law is clear on the matter: she must be stoned to death. Then they ask him what he has to say about the matter, seeking to trap him between law and justice. When you think about it, several questions emerge: Why is she there alone? Where is her partner in adultery? Is it just that only one of the two guilty parties should face punishment?

Then there is the woman herself. Try to imagine her terror and shame, standing there before the legal authorities, a victim of both the law and a sexist society. Ask yourself whether she is hoping against hope that Jesus will somehow save her from a terrible death. Won't Jesus, of all, people show her compassion? But the law is clear: she must be stoned. The authorities think they have Jesus in a trap.

In the story, Jesus stoops down and writes on the ground with his finger. Then he stands up and tells her accusers, "He that is without sin among you, let him first cast a stone at her" (John 8:7b). Then he stoops down again and writes some more. As he writes, the crowd, beginning with the eldest, drifts away until only Jesus and the woman are left there alone.

All the accusers in the crowd left because none of them were without sin. As I apply this story to recovery, I would phrase it to say that none of us are without mistakes and weaknesses. Perfection eludes us all. In my depression, I can turn almost anything into a mistake. But even if my mistakes really are mistakes, I am far from the only one in the world making them. If I deserve to be stoned, then so does everybody else.

This is the reality of the human situation. By treating myself as the greatest of all sinners, the King Kong of sin, I'm being arrogant, holding myself to a standard higher than the standard of other mortals. When I remember this Bible story, I am able to ease up on the self-punishment and move toward self-acceptance. Yes, I need to own my real mistakes and to make amends as well as I can. No, I don't need to beat myself up incessantly about each mistake. They are a part of what it is to be human. Why would I beat myself up for that?

A PERFECT LIFE

There is a story about a medieval Spanish monk who believed he had found a strategy to lead a life without sin, a life that ensured him of going to heaven. Here is his strategy: "I am confident that, after my death, I will go to heaven because I have never made a decision on my own. I have always followed the orders of my superiors. If I erred, the sin is theirs, not mine." To me, what the monk lacks in a willingness to take responsibility he makes up for in being passive-aggressive.

Leaving aside the question of whether it's possible to avoid responsibility by saying, "I was just obeying orders," I would ask whether the monk's strategy offers a real counterexample to the point that we all make mistakes in our lives. The answer hinges on another question: did this monk, who sought to never make a decision on his own, really have a genuine human life? The answer is easy: no, he didn't. By giving up his freedom to decide for himself, his agency in determining his own life, he also gave up what it means to live fully as a human being.

As we've seen, our self-esteem and self-respect grow as we make our own decisions. Since we are fallible human beings, some of these decisions are inevitably going to be bad ones. The mistakes we make are the cost of recovery. We need the courage to make mistakes. In *Healing the Shame That Binds You*, John Bradshaw writes, "Being human requires courage. It requires courage because being human is being imperfect."[22] Step by step, as we make our own decisions while accepting our human fallibility, our courage grows and our recovery moves forward.

IGNORANCE

There's an interchange early in the movie *Independence Day* that clarifies what it means to be a flawed human being making decisions. The earth is being invaded by extraterrestrials. Some believe there is a connection between this invasion and an alien space craft that allegedly crashed years previously at a site in New Mexico known as Area 51. The president (Bill Pullman), along with computer scientist David Levinson (Jeff Goldblum) and his father Julius (Judd Hirsch), learns the truth about Area 51 from Albert Nimziki (James Rebhorn), the secretary of defense.

> Julius Levinson: AAAHHH, don't give me unprepared! You knew about this for years! What, with that spaceship you found in New Mexico! What was it called . . . Roswell, New Mexico! And that other place . . . uh . . . Area 51, Area 51! You knew then! And you did nothing.
>
> President Thomas Whitmore: Mr. Levinson, contrary to what you may have read in the tabloids, there is no Area 51. There is no space-ship . . .
>
> Albert Nimziki: Uh . . . excuse me, Mr. President? That's not entirely accurate.
>
> David Levinson: What, which part?[23]

There were many things President Whitmore didn't know. "That's not entirely accurate" is an enormous understatement. When we watched the movie on the psych unit, it broke us up. Turns out there is an Area 51, there is a spaceship, and, as the president is soon going to learn, there is even an extraterrestrial in the spaceship. Fortunately, this new knowledge doesn't come too late for him to devise a plan and make decisions that will ultimately save Earth.

Compared with President Whitmore, we are both lucky and unlucky. Lucky because we are not charged with making decisions to save Earth from an invasion; unlucky because we are charged with making decisions in the midst of our own lives and there's nobody like Albert Nimziki to tell us what we need to know so those decisions are good ones. We have to make our decisions with what we know at the time, which is most likely a combination of knowledge and ignorance.

This being true, we treat ourselves unjustly when we are hyper–self-critical of our mistakes. I used to exhaust myself trying to decide how someone might react to something I did or said. Try as I might—and I tried really, really hard—in the end I was still guessing. When I guessed wrong, I would beat up on myself and apologize far beyond what was necessary.

I'm a flawed human being, who is not in possession of all the relevant facts. Yet my humanity depends on my making decisions. Given the tension of these realities, it is cruel and inhuman of me to beat up on myself when some of those decisions turn out to be bad ones. Forgiveness is a far better option.

Help 21

Learning Compassion

In different ways, several of the recent Helps have been about compassion. Sometimes it's compassion toward ourselves: the need in recovery to forgive ourselves, to be gentle with ourselves, to accept our human limits and not judge or beat up on ourselves. Sometimes it's compassion toward other people, granting them this same understanding.

I have a story about compassion. Every other week or so, I visit an elderly man in a local health care center where I am a volunteer. Sometimes he's taking a nap when I arrive. I don't want to wake him. Besides, with his hearing aids out, I'd probably need to set off a small to midsize bomb to get him to open his eyes. I wait around for a while, and then, if he doesn't wake up, I leave him a note and go home.

I walk back to my car—I had parked a whole block away!—muttering to myself about wasted time. But once I get that frustration out of my system, I can at least give myself credit for trying to see him. I can also imagine his getting pleasure from reading my note. The next time I find him awake, I know he'll tell me he's sorry he missed me and thank me for the note and for taking the time to come by. In spite of his being asleep, I accomplished something after all. Of course, in the future I can also do some real-world things like call ahead and check with an aide to see whether he's awake or asleep. But honestly, this feels too much like work, and I'm a volunteer.

A week or so goes by, and I go to see him again. No, I haven't called in advance, but I am coming right after lunch in the hope that I'll catch him before he takes a nap. Bingo! He's wide awake, shaving with his early-model electric razor. When he's finished, I help him unplug the cord from the far wall, roll it up so it doesn't take up much space, and then put the razor away in the top drawer of his nightstand. That done, we start talking about how the week has been for each of us. For a man whose life is mostly confined to a single large building, he has a surprising number of interesting things to talk about.

First, he told me about a trip he'd taken the afternoon before with a group of other residents from the health care center to a Minnesota Twins game. He was grateful for the trip, made even better because the Twins had won. He was also grateful for the hot dog a staff member had bought for him at the game, a treat, but he had never had that kind of spicy ketchup before, another new thing in the world. I didn't have the heart to tell him that I put mustard on my hot dogs and have no use for ketchup, spicy or otherwise.

Then he moved on to tell me about what had happened the previous day, after an aide had rolled him out to the front porch, so he could enjoy some fresh air. While he was sitting there, two young deer had come down the street, not more than ten yards from him. He said they were just walking along, like they were having a little chat, unbothered by him sitting there watching them. When they got to the far corner of the building, they turned, so he lost sight of them. Just to the north of the building and through a little fringe of woods, there's a beautiful lake. Probably they had turned to go down there, maybe to continue their stroll along the sandy shore. My elderly friend became animated as he told the story. Obviously he had been thrilled to see the deer and he was excited to tell me about it.

It was a good story, another one of those interesting things that always seem to be happening to him. He paused for a moment, and I thought he had something else he wanted to tell me about, but he wasn't finished with the two deer. "You know," he said, "deer hooves aren't really that hard. Walking on pavement can hurt them. I hope they didn't do any serious damage to themselves before they left the street and went down to the lake."

These are simple words, yet they demonstrate a profound understanding of life. I've read books about compassion, some very good ones, but none of them felt as natural as this man's concern about the deer and their vulnerable hooves. With a simple story, he had given me a treasure, shown me what lies at the heart of compassion. Remembering how his face looked as he talked, I believe his compassion drew him away from the toll that a long life had taken, away from confinement in an institution, toward two creatures he was likely never to see again. He gave himself up to compassion, and compassion gave him a blessing.

I hope that some of his compassion has rubbed off on me, and I have become more like him. When I follow his example—letting go of what weighs on me and letting myself be drawn toward something outside myself, like two young deer or an elderly friend in a health care center—I am brought to a better and healthier place in my life.

Help 22

Finding What's Life-Giving

AFTER I HAD SERVED two churches as a three-month sabbatical-supply pastor, I decided to take training to serve as an interim pastor, a position that normally lasts from one to two years. My therapist, psychiatrist, and family all agreed this was a safe decision. Overall, my interim work has gone well, which is not to say that interim jobs are easy.

In reality, being an interim pastor means serving a church in a challenging time of transition. If the former pastor has left on the best of terms (retiring or moving on after a productive pastorate), then it's a time of grief over the loss of someone who will be missed. If the former pastor has left on not so good terms (the pastor and the parish were a bad match or there was a serious breach of trust), then the grief could be mixed with anger, guilt, and disappointment.

So positive or negative, these endings soak up a lot of energy, leaving congregations tired and depleted as the interim time begins, just the opposite of what's needed. In my faith tradition, ministers are not appointed by a bishop; they are chosen by a vote of the congregation. This means the church must go through a period of self-study and discernment, select a search committee, and then support that committee as it seeks applications, narrows the field, conducts interviews, makes a selection, and finally brings the candidate to the whole congregation for a vote.

With so much to do, it's easy to see why the process takes so long. With such an important choice to make, this is obviously not a good time for a church to be at low energy. As the interim I'm faced with the task of getting people fired up to work hard just when they're running on empty. Thanks a lot!

From my training as an interim, I've learned that asking members to share their favorite church stories can help them to reenergize. No demands, no expectations—just tell a story. Like hungry church mice pouring out of the woodwork, once the stories get started, it's hard to stop them. I've seen this happen a number of times, and it is always wonderful to see people come alive as they tell their stories.

I start by asking people to share funny stories. There's always somebody who gets us started, and then the stories just keep coming. At one church, an elderly woman couldn't keep from laughing as she told the story of a church potluck where everybody had brought baked beans. Through her laughter, she struggled to tell us that because of the beans, the after-dinner program had needed to be shortened. In another church, I learned that because of the custodian's shopping error, bread and prune juice had been served for communion. That emptied the church even faster than the all-bean dinner! Church dinners, communion mishaps, shocking bulletin misprints, animals that have invaded church—dogs, cats, bats, rats, a swarm of bees—the stories keep coming. People start leaning forward, not wanting to miss anything, and the energy begins to flow.

From the funny stories, we move on to more serious ones. This is usually a little slower getting started, and I might ask someone ahead of time to prime the pump. But again, once the stories get going, they keep coming. Many of these stories are about how the church has been there for people: brought in meals after a death or during an illness, provided companionship and support through a challenging time, given respite to an exhausted caregiver, offered acceptance and a welcome when no one else would. These are powerful stories, and they create energy that the church needs for the work ahead.

Just as stories can be life giving and energizing for churches, so they can also be life giving and energizing for us in recovery. We can start with short funny stories, one-off events, anecdotes—the equivalent to the baked-beans and prune-juice church stories. For example, if the time and audience is right (no children and nobody easily shocked), I love to tell the story about the time I was preaching on the importance of perseverance, about running the race that God has set before us. I wanted a strong ending and I settled on, "Don't give up. God is with you. Keep on trucking."

OK, I'm not saying this ending would make it into a book of all-time great sermons, but it would give me a powerful conclusion, especially if I pumped up the volume, a preacher's trick to make what we're saying sound important. But my lips got tangled, and I said *fucking* instead of *trucking*. I got the words wrong, but I did do a really good job of upping the volume.

Still I might have gotten away with it if I'd just kept talking. People would have been left to wonder whether they had really heard what they thought they had heard, and I could have preserved a shred of deniability. Unfortunately, I was so shocked by what I had said that I automatically slapped myself in the mouth. You don't see that in the pulpit every day!

For years and years afterward, some merciless church members would come up to me, say, "Keep on trucking, Bob," and then burst out laughing. Of course, when I first realized what I'd said and done, I wanted to dig a hole under the pulpit and climb in. But over time and with the ongoing recovery of humor and self-acceptance, I've come to love this story. Now I tell it on myself, and I'm the one who laughs the hardest and longest.

As it is with church stories, funny personal stories like this one are the easiest to share. But again, like church stories, I am also able to share serious, at times painful stories in the hope that they will be life giving. Sometimes it's simply that I'm with people I trust, so I choose to share part of myself, knowing it will bring us still closer together.

Sometimes I tell these stories to help someone else. For example, with a clergy friend who was having trouble finding her next job, I shared my own stories of job searches that came up empty, including the painful ones where I really wanted the position. I did this to let her know that's she's not alone in her failure and that there's nothing shameful about not getting every job you apply for. I could have told her some truisms about job hunting and church search committee dynamics, but I helped her a lot more by sharing a story from my own life.

I invite you to share your own stories. Start with whichever ones are easiest and most fun to tell, and you'll have your own experience of how life giving it can be to tell stories. Tell one, and you'll want to tell another. Let the stories flow. Just keep on trucking.

HELP 23

Staying Oriented

As THE NEW INTERIM pastor at a church in a small town in western Minnesota, I spent my first day in the parsonage opening boxes and figuring out where to put things. Living in a parsonage was a new experience for me, and this was a great house with a double garage on a large corner lot. We'd kept our home in the Twin Cities, and Sue would come visit me on weekends. In the meantime, the place was all mine.

I didn't realize until summer that living in a corner house on a large lot has a downside. I got to live in the house (great!), but I also got to cut the grass. The soil is extremely fertile in this part of western Minnesota. At the height of the growing season, I needed to harvest the grass every four or five days. Moreover, this was the parsonage, and everybody knew it. If I didn't keep the yard looking good, people would talk.

But all the yard care lay in the future. On my first day living there, I made good progress with the unpacking. By early evening, I needed a break and some supper, so I grabbed my coat and set out to explore my new hometown. I stopped at a Burger King for a quick meal and found a slightly used newspaper to read while I ate. Well-fed and at peace with the world, I left the restaurant and just wandered around town, a free spirit checking things out.

This is all about as innocent as it can get, so I was surprised when a police car pulled up behind me. I was even more surprised when the officer inside turned the car's spotlight on me. Only then did I realize that I'd been walking in the street, not right down the middle but off to one side—still, undeniably in the street. And true, there was a sidewalk, but I'd gotten used to being on the edge of the street when I was a runner, and for some reason that's where I was walking. I really hadn't been paying much attention.

The officer was nice enough in a no-nonsense sort of way. He asked me my name, and I nailed it. Then he asked me where I lived, a bit of a problem. Of course I knew that I lived in the parsonage, and I knew that it was diagonally across the town square from the church, but I was new and hadn't paid attention to the exact street, not to mention the house number. Complicating matters, I don't have the world's best sense of direction. When I pointed to where I thought I lived, for all I knew I could have been pointing to the town dump. Hey, it's a small town, and I could have found my way home—eventually. I was just a little disoriented.

To complicate matters still more, as I talked to the officer, I looked down and realized that the old coat I'd put on was misbuttoned. It happens. I'm not the world's neatest dresser. No law broken, but I did look kind of like a derelict. Furthermore, as I talked, I licked my lips and came away with a distinct taste of ketchup. OK, I'm not the world's neatest eater either. Again no law broken, but not the way to inspire confidence. I told the officer I was the new pastor in town. Right—and he's the king of Siam.

Things were going downhill fast. I didn't know the laws about vagrancy, but I suspected I was getting close to qualifying. In desperation I started telling him about the search committee that had hired me for my new job. Bingo! Turns out, he knew most of them, an advantage of living in a small town. He smiled and said he was just worried when he saw me walking in the street. I told him I understood and that I'd always use the sidewalk in the future. I've mostly kept my word.

This is one of those stories I love to tell. When the opportunity arises and I can fit this story in—I confess that sometimes I kind of jam it into a conversation even when it doesn't really fit—I lean forward, slide into full story-telling mode, and start talking, taking my time, including every detail, never forgetting the ketchup and the creatively buttoned coat. As with the church stories I encourage members to tell, sharing this story is energizing. Being able to tell the story says something about the progress of my recovery. I can truly say that telling it is life giving.

Beyond telling of the minimal embarrassment of being stopped by a police officer when I wasn't dressed for success, this disorientation story costs me very little. I have other disorientation stories, set in the depth of my depression that cost me a fortune. They include many variants on the basic story of lying in bed, too exhausted and too afraid to start the day. I have stories of walking around, even at times driving around, so trapped in my racing thoughts that I literally did not know where I was or what

I was doing. I have stories of conversations with people at church when I had no idea what I was supposed to say next. I'd lost the script of how conversations were supposed to happen. I have the story of being in the ER, overwhelmed by pain, lost in depression.

I use my stories to help others living with mental illness. I also use them as a point of orientation in my own recovery. The most powerful of them, the ER story, was the ground zero of my meltdown. I look back to it and see how far I have come in recovery, not measured in miles but in increased well-being. I believe progress begets progress. When I see how far I have come, I have confidence that I can go still further. I may be a little fuzzy about how to get back to the parsonage, but I'm quite certain that I'm moving forward in the direction of recovery.

Help 24

Enduring No Longer

How much is enough? If you drink coffee, I bet one cup is not enough. But when do you stop? Will two cups do it? Maybe three or four? I bet ten cups will leave you jumping up and down. Likewise, with dessert—one slice of chocolate cake? Sure, that would be great, thank you. Would you like another piece? Well, if you insist. It really is great cake. Three, four? Want to eat the whole damn cake? At some point it's just too much. What was a good thing, maybe a wonderful thing, flips and becomes the opposite.

This flipping to the opposite is not limited to coffee, cake, or whatever else is on the menu. For people recovering from mental illness, the ability to endure is often cited as a virtue. Well, of course it is. Isn't it? The capacity to endure pain and frustration for a time is essential when therapy feels stuck and the meds aren't helping, the doctor's office doesn't call back, reimbursement is denied, or you spend all day filling out the wrong form, though it's the one that you were given. There are many speed bumps on the way to recovery. If you give up the first time you hit one, you'll never get where you're going. When the bump is bad, you need help. You need someone beside you to keep you from quitting when illness and bureaucracy make it hard to go on.

This is true, but it's also true that endurance taken too far can do us harm, a reality that was brought home to me unexpectedly while I was watching the movie *Dr. Zhivago*. The title character (Omar Sharif) says, "Even Comrade Lenin underestimated both the anguish of that nine hundred mile-long front and our cursed capacity for suffering."[24] The nine hundred mile-long front has receded into history, but our "cursed capacity for suffering" is still with us.

We see this in many aspects of recovery. For example, putting up with some awkwardness and false starts with a new therapist is usually a good thing. Building a therapeutic alliance takes time, and changing one's therapist can be a pain. But how much of a good thing can it be to go on and on with a therapist when you're not getting anywhere or when you feel the therapist is being disrespectful? It's far better to recognize that this can happen for any number of reasons and to change therapists rather than endure a therapist who isn't helping.

What's true of enduring an unhelpful therapist is equally true with an unhelpful medication. Yes, of course, give the medication the time, the three weeks or whatever the doctor says it needs. But please, if the medication becomes more than you can handle alone, get help so that you can endure until the waiting time is over. If that time is past, if you're a month or more into the new med or adjusted dosage and you don't feel better or the side effects are intolerable, it's time to stop enduring and to seek a change.

Therapists and meds—talk and pills—are two key elements of recovery where endurance can flip from a positive to a negative. The same can be true of therapeutic groups, trial work periods, housing arrangements, insurance plans, and other areas of one's recovery. There's so much in our lives where the ability to endure starts as a good thing and then it isn't good.

In negotiating questions of when to endure and when to stop, there is much help in Reinhold Niebuhr's Serenity Prayer. My favorite version is one used by Alcoholics Anonymous.

> God grant us the serenity to accept the things we cannot change,
>> Courage to change the things we can,
>> And the wisdom to know the difference.[25]

Many of us are struggling against alcoholism and other addictions, struggles that are endured one day at a time. Many of us are living with physical health conditions that can't be changed, at least not yet, and every day we ask for the serenity to accept what can't be changed. Some of the consequences of our mental illness and its treatment can't be changed, at least not yet, and recovery means learning to live with these consequences.

On the other hand, when we try to endure the things that can be changed, suffering when it's not necessary, we stifle our recovery. Society encourages us to endure this pointless suffering by telling us to "tough it out" and "suck it up." For me trying to tough it out, trying to endure without asking for help, trying to stuff pain when there was nowhere left to stuff it, got me a narrow bed on a locked ward. When I hear these words now, I hear my mental illness being minimized, not taken seriously. These words tell me that mental illness is my fault and that if I were a better, stronger person, I'd be fine. The name for this is *stigma*. It makes mental illness much worse.

I don't listen to these words anymore. I don't intend to endure pain when it can be changed. If I don't know whether something can be changed, if I don't have the wisdom to tell the difference between what I must endure and what I can change, I've learned that I need to talk with people I trust who know what I'm facing. Maybe we decide that what's hurting can't be changed. Then I will need their help to endure it. OK, that's just the way life is sometimes. But maybe something can be changed, and I'm suffering what I don't have to. Then, with all the help I can get, I'll do my best to change it.

HELP 25

Practicing Resilience

I LEARNED AN IMPORTANT recovery lesson on an Atlantic beach in North Carolina. One sunny morning, my wife and I were out with old friends collecting pretty rocks, sea shells, and sand dollars. Finding a gold doubloon or two would have been nice, but my ability to accept reality has increased in recovery, so I wasn't counting on it. I had found my first sand dollar and was heading for another when one of our friends yelled, "Be careful! Not every white circle in the sand is a sand dollar." And with that she pointed upward to all the seagulls that were circling over us.

A life lesson—sand dollars turn into seagull poop; dreams turn into dust—there is no way to escape disappointments. Those of us living with mental illness are experts in the field of disappointment. We didn't set out seeking mental illness. We had hopes and dreams before mental illness snatched them away from us. Disappointment has become our new normal.

In recovery, we want our dreams back, but we don't want to set ourselves up for yet more pain. Resilience enables us to do this, to move forward in the face of possible disappointment. It is the ability not to let the seagull poop stop you from looking for the sand dollars. You see a white circle and get your hopes up, but then your sand dollar turns out to be poop. Being resilient means you don't give up. Maybe you vent with an expletive, but you keep looking. You know that any white circle in the sand could go either way. That's reality. You are able to accept it and move on.

Resilience requires that we think clearly and act realistically. In recovery I have learned that my depression feeds on my tendency to overgeneralize and catastrophize, transforming a little bit of something bad into a great catastrophe. The heating bill is higher than we expected. That's reality. But then the cascade of disasters starts: *I know the electricity bill is going to be twice what it was last month. Oh my God, tomorrow we'll get a letter that the interest rate on our mortgage is going up. No, it's worse. They're going to cancel our mortgage! We don't have the money to pay it off. They're going to take away our home. It's terrible! I'm so afraid and so ashamed! What can I do? I have to do something right now! What can I do?*

This is how overgeneralization and catastrophizing worked for me. In the language of cognitive behavioral therapy (CBT), these are "cognitive distortions." They are ways of thinking that do not map reality, that yield negative feelings in which depression can flourish. In sand dollar terms, these cognitive distortions would have us believe that every white circle on the beach is courtesy of a seagull. CBT teaches that we need to thank sea gulls for only some of them. As a matter of fact, that white circle over there is a sand dollar, a perfect one. In my depression, all I see is poop; in recovery, I see that only some of what's out there is poop. We call this progress.

Resilience avoids both the false negativity of these cognitive distortions and the false positivity of wishful thinking. What we've learned from our mental illness can help us here. We've been disappointed far too often to move forward without a strong dose of reality. We've learned the hard way that wishing doesn't make it so and that there will always be some poop in the future. We keep looking because we've learned there really are some sand dollars out there. Some white circles are, some aren't—we know the score.

When I learned the lesson about white circles in the sand, I was not out on the beach by myself. My wife, our friends, and I shared our successes and failures: "Hey, I just found a perfect sand dollar!" "Lucky you. Can you believe this circle of seagull poop was so perfect that it faked me out until I bent over and got a good look at it?" We encouraged one another to keep looking. We knew that at the end of the day we would admire our sand dollars together and together curse the circles of poop that had led us astray.

I've learned that resilience thrives when we are not alone. I believe that it's possible to practice resilience by oneself, but having people around is a huge help. "How to Make Stress Your Friend," a much-viewed *TED Talk* by Kelly McGonigal,[26] does a wonderful job of establishing the link between resilience and other people, as well as the biology that underlies that link.

What I call my "second career" (the sabbatical supplies and the interims) has been a laboratory in resilience. Since I returned to work, I've held ten church positions. I didn't keep an exact count, but I bet I applied for at least another dozen positions that I didn't get. Applying for jobs has been much like hunting for sand dollars.

Whether I find a sand dollar or seagull poop, I always talk with someone about my job search. If I get the job, we celebrate responsibly; if I don't get it, we talk through the disappointment. I know that if I keep the failure to myself, I'll brood over the loss and start blaming myself. By doing that, I'm inviting depression back into my life. On the other hand, if I talk about the situation with a colleague, I receive help in keeping the disappointment in perspective, and I don't start personalizing. Instead of going inward, I go outward toward reality: nobody gets every job; disappointment is built into my line of work. Rather than blame myself for failure, let's see if there's anything that can be learned that will help me get the next job I apply for. Who knows? It might even pay better.

If I ever go back to that beach in North Carolina, of course I'm going to look for sand dollars, and I might even look up at the sky and thank the sea gulls for the lesson they taught me. On second thought, I'm not sure that this is a good idea, especially if there are other people around who could hear me. What I'm sure I would do is remember how much of my recovery is due to learning resilience. As I rewrite this Help yet again (this must be version ten or eleven), I can feel the resilience kicking in and that keeps me going.

HELP 26

Letting Go of Denial

"DENIAL AIN'T JUST A river in Egypt" is a phrase I first heard from AA folks on the psych unit, but my acquaintance with denial goes back much earlier in my life than that. My mom practiced denial in things great and small. Sadly, this included denying any need to go the doctor, an unreality that may well have cost her years of life. Denial says that what you don't know (or at least don't admit) can't hurt you. Keep the problem hidden, never bring it up, and all will be well. If you deny it, it will all just go away—except that it doesn't.

An ostrich with his head stuck in the ground is the classic image of denial. I use *his* because I identify with the image. By the time I was hospitalized, I had not been to a doctor in more than three decades. As I made progress in recovery, learning to let go of the punishing scenarios in my head in favor of the reality out in the world, it became increasingly hard for me to deny the reality of my own body and its need to be cared for. Calling the doctor, acknowledging that I have a real body in the real world, loomed as a major step in getting real and getting well.

My resistance to making this call almost defeated me. I felt so ashamed of my cowardice for not having had the fortitude to do what many other adults do on a regular basis, at least those fortunate enough to have health insurance. By this point I had convinced myself that I had serious health problems and that they were all my fault. I could hear the doctor saying, "Oh, Bob, I'm so sorry. If you'd just come in a little earlier, all would have been OK. But you put it off too long, and now—uh, well, I'm sorry—but you'd better get your affairs in order. There's not much time. By the way, would you pay your bill on the way out?" I can joke about it now, but then I was terrified.

After promising my therapist and using every fiber of will I could summon, I made an appointment. Immediately I was tempted to cancel it, but I had promised that I would do this. I also had my wife's strong support and encouragement, and I just couldn't let her down again. I went to the doctor, and I'm proud of myself for going. I want to repeat how proud I am of myself for going, an awesome victory over my depression. And the visit turned out to be a big anticlimax. I was fine. He just gave me some advice to eat less and exercise more. I've been somewhat erratic in following this wise advice, but I've been totally consistent in having annual physicals for the fourteen years or so since that doctor's visit.

If you've been denying yourself medical care, I urge you to call your doctor. If you don't have a doctor, get helping in finding one. If necessary, get help in finding out how to pay for one. This is serious. I've heard a number of times that people living with mental illness die twenty-five years sooner than the average person. Do not let mental illness steal years from your life.

Besides denying the need to go to the doctor, my mom taught me a more sweeping kind of denial. I imagine her with her hands over her ears so she wouldn't have to hear anything that might be upsetting—very much a sister to the ostrich with his head stuck in the ground. Far more by her expression and emotional reaction than by actual words, she taught me not to talk about anything that would worry her or cause her anxiety.

A kid bullying me at school, a math class where I felt over my head, a turndown the first time I called a girl for a date—I learned to keep these things to myself and to bury them as deeply as possible. Over time, I just did this automatically. Things still bothered me; I couldn't control that. But I certainly could control talking with anybody about my problems, which is as close as I could come to denying that these things ever happened.

Beginning with my time in the hospital, I started to open up about things that bothered me. Sometimes they came out with a lot of shame and grief, but I was no longer denying they were there. Therapy continued this process until now I'm able to talk almost naturally with friends about things that I once would have been quick to deny. I've learned that this is what you do with friends. You share the bad with the good, and you let that sharing be the glue that holds your friendship together. Maybe this is easy for some people, but I've had to work at it.

Now I want to say a good word about ostriches. I've learned that ostriches have been the victims of slander and malicious lies. The reality is that they aren't feathered deniers who stick their heads in the sand when trouble looms. Why would they? A full-grown ostrich stands about 9 feet tall, weighs about 350 pounds, has a top speed of 40 miles an hour, and can kill a lion with one swift kick. Depending on the threat, the ostrich is well equipped for either fight or flight.

The idea that ostriches stick their heads in the ground may come from the fact that they dig massive holes to lay their eggs in. The male and the female take turns sitting on the eggs, periodically sticking their heads down in the hole to check on the eggs or to move them around. If you see ostriches doing this, you might think they were trying to hide from something, but this isn't the case at all. Sticking their heads in the ground isn't about denial; it's about being good parents.

If anything, ostriches are poster birds for recovery, not for denial. With their strength and competence, they stand for our own ability to deal effectively with reality. In recovery, we claim the abilities that are ours and we learn to push back against denial, not allowing it to continue to distort and minimize our lives. We don't need denial any more than the formidable ostrich needs to hide its head in the sand.

I don't want to blame my mom for teaching me denial. I suspect that she learned denial from her parents. She was kind and tried hard to be a good mom, but denial tripped her up. She feared anything outside of the little world that she was trying so hard to control, and she missed out on so much because of that. I've lived with this kind of fear, and I can testify to all the life that it costs. I can also testify that there is a much better way to live.

Help 27

Listening and Noticing

I ONCE VISITED AN elderly parishioner in a nursing home who told me stories about his mother. As a girl, she had been taught to whistle while accompanying herself on the piano. Like drawing and Latin, whistling was part of the school curriculum. He told me that being able to whistle in tune had been a source of pleasure for her all her life.

In my mind's eye I see her—thin, white hair in a tight bun, carefully dressed, sitting erect—playing an old hymn and whistling reverently in solemn harmony. Though she can't see them, bands of angels are hovering around her head. Then she stops, turns around, and carefully scans the parlor, making sure that she is all alone and that the doors and windows are fully closed. She turns back to the piano, takes a breath, and launches into a hot Scott Joplin rag, whistling for all she's worth, trying to keep up with the piano. Grinning and pushing their halos back, the angels start dancing to the ragtime beat.

Of course, I don't know whether this whistling mother was ever so daring or whether angels really started dancing around her head, but I hope so. At any rate, just the thought of her playing ragtime and whistling along brightens my day and gives me a charge of pleasure. And who knows? Maybe she didn't whistle Scott Joplin, maybe her taste ran more toward Led Belly or Jelly Roll Morton. I wonder what kind of dance the angels did when she played their music.

I wish I could stop here, stop after sharing a wonderful story and playing with it a little, but what happened when I visited my parishioner is more complicated. He told me several other stories that I can't remember. They may also have been truly wonderful stories, even better than this one about his mother, but I don't know. I hadn't listened to those stories.

The visit where I learned about his mother took place shortly before my first hospitalization, when it was becoming impossible for me to attend to anything that was going on outside my mind. For much of the visit, I might as well have been sitting in the room by myself. Instead of listening to his stories, my mind was totally engaged in scenarios of my life at its most shameful and cringe-worthy point, scenarios that were running on the screen right behind my eyeballs.

These shame-drenched scenarios were enlivened by spurts of anxiety: *I'm so behind. I shouldn't have tried to fit in this visit. I have no idea what to say on Sunday. Why do I always put things off? I'm a phony. I don't deserve this job. I'm taking the job away from somebody else who could do it a lot better than I. If I don't get my act together, people are going to start yelling at me. I just can't do it anymore. I can't stand to live like this!*

I'm grateful that on this particular visit in the nursing home something happened to interrupt the scenes playing in my mind. I don't remember what it was that jolted me back to paying attention—maybe my anxiety about all I had to do caused me to sneak a look at my watch, maybe an announcement on the PA, maybe my parishioner noticed I wasn't paying attention and raised his voice. I only know something pulled my attention away from my internal big screen and back to him, and I'm so glad it did. Coming back to real life, I not only had a brief respite from shame and anxiety, but I also had the good fortune to hear the story about his mother and her whistling.

I don't want to miss any more good stories. In recovery, I'm learning to take my focus off the internal movie screen and put it on the world around me. I am better able to take in what's going on, hear the stories and to notice the little things. My friend Margery Leveen Sher, author of *The Noticer's Guide to Living and Laughing*, writes,

> Noticing is mindfulness, with a smile. Being attentive to the world around you, and living in the moment. And it means seeing the pleasure and the humor that's right in front of your nose. Taking delight in Noticing what you see.[27]

If you're open to the world right in front of your nose, taking in its pleasure and humor, then you're not stuck in your mind, attending to your shame and anxiety. It's the difference between walking down the street noticing what you see—blooming flowers, birds at a feeder, a quarter that somebody dropped, a little child on a swing, a garden gnome scowling in the weeds—and walking down the street oblivious to all except your own self-punitive thoughts.

It can be hard to get outside your mind and to escape the ever-repeating scenarios. But once you start looking and listening, the energy and surprise of life around you will keep pulling you outward, away from toxic self-absorption. Our senses are part of this outward pull, forever drawing us into the world around us. There is so much life to experience, and it's so easy to find. Just notice what's right in front of your nose.

It wasn't that long after this nursing home visit that my parishioner died. I never got around to asking him whether he had ever caught his mom whistling while playing Scott Joplin, Led Belly, or Jelly Roll Morton in the parlor. My guess is that he hadn't. And even if he had, he might have felt that he owed it to his mom's memory to keep her more raucous whistling a secret. He was that kind of a person, and I tell this story in honor of him.

Help 28

Living One's Faith in Recovery

IN WRITING ABOUT FAITH and recovery, I want to be careful and respectful of those living with mental illness who are not part of a religious tradition or whose tradition is different from my own. I believe that we need all the help we can get in recovery and that religious tradition is a great help for many of us. The best way I can do this is to stay close to my tradition. I invite you to take from my experience whatever you find helpful.

In *The Noonday Demon*, Andrew Solomon writes,

> Religion provides answers to unanswerable questions. It cannot usually pull people out of depression; indeed, even the most religious people find that their faith thins or vanishes during the depths of depression. It can, however, defend against the complaint, and it can help people to survive depressive episodes.[28]

These observations are true to my story. When my depression was at its worst, all that was good and sustaining in my faith disappeared, leaving only the pain of religious failure to add to all of the other pain. I used this as yet another big stick to beat myself up with: *"What kind of Christian are you?" "Why don't you just accept forgiveness and get over it?" "What part of hypocrite do you fail to understand?" "Who wants to come to a church with a depressed minister?" "Whatever faith is, I don't want yours." "Man, you are sure in the wrong line of work."*

The suffering that these thoughts caused me—like so much of the pain of depression—was self-inflicted. No other pastor or church member, no one in the hospital, no one I've ever met who is living with mental illness, no mental health professional has ever accused me of being some kind of religious failure, a faux pastor, or a hypocrite. On the contrary, because I have suffered and been honest about it, people have told me that I am just the kind of minister they've been looking for. I can hear that now, but for a long time, I could not get beyond shame and self-disgust.

Solomon showed me that the issue was not the content of my faith but the depth of my depression. As the disease took away whatever joy and satisfaction life had brought me, it also took away the consolation and the meaning my faith had given me. In the worst times, I believed I had failed God, just like I'd failed my church, my family, and everybody else. As Solomon writes, this is what depression does to faith. To beat myself up about my failing faith is to give depression the victory. I refuse to do this.

Maybe you disagree with Solomon; maybe your faith didn't disappear when your depression was at its worst. If you are of my tradition, maybe our affirmation of the unconditional love of God revealed in Jesus Christ stayed with you, helped you survive the worst and sustained your self-worth in the face of depression's attempt to shatter it. If you are of another tradition, maybe you found within its affirmations something so powerful that it allowed you to withstand depression at its most malevolent. If so, I honor your story, even as I ask you to honor mine.

My story is one of experiencing the loss of faith Solomon describes and then, in my own way, coming back to faith. Finding my way back was inseparable from my daily scripture readings. Though at first they were a means to find structure amidst the chaos of depression, over time they became more than this. As I recovered my ability to read with understanding, the content of these readings began to seep into me, especially the daily readings in the Book of Psalms. My return to faith has primarily been through this ancient portal, and this is the story I want to share with you.

I'll start with the first verses of Psalm 69:

> Save me, O God; for the waters are come in unto my soul.

> I sink in deep mire, where there is no standing: I am come into deep waters, where the floods overflow me. I am weary of my crying: my throat is dried: mine eyes fail while I wait for my God. (Psalm 69:1–3)

Psalm 69 is what scholars call a "lament"; about one-third of the 150 psalms are laments. The psalms, which were written more than two and a half millennia ago, have different authors. In my thirty years of ministry before I was hospitalized, I never paid much attention to them, but they were there when I needed them. Reading verses such as these from Psalm 69 post-hospitalization brought deep healing. Phrases such as "sink in deep mire," "the floods overflow me," and "weary of my crying" could have been spoken by me in the depths of my depression. When you can talk about something, it no longer controls you. The psalm gave me words to talk about my depression, words that were adequate to the pain that my depression was causing me.

Take just one verse from another lament: "I am weary with my groaning; all the night make I my bed to swim; I water my couch with my tears." (Psalm 6:6) Again these are words true to the anguish and hopelessness of depression. It's as if the psalmist who wrote them thousands of years ago knew exactly how I was feeling. So many people don't understand, but this ancient writer understood perfectly, assuring me that I am not alone.

What's more—these psalms are in the Bible, along with all the other scriptures that we read in worship. I find this to be amazing. The temptation to deny pain is great, but the Bible is honest about it. Our suffering is not rejected; we have a home in sacred story. As we fight stigma, seek to stand against those who would shame us for our illness, the Bible stands with us.

These psalms are honest about the worst times and places of our lives, but they do not leave us there. As in Psalm 40, there is movement out of the pit.

> I waited patiently for the Lord; and he inclined unto me, and heard my cry.
> He brought me up also out of an horrible pit, out of the miry clay, and set my feet upon a rock, and established my goings.
> And he hath put a new song in my mouth, even praise unto our God. (Psalm 40:1–3a)

The laments move from honesty about despair to hope for a better future, where God will put "a new song in my mouth." Part of Psalm 30 echoes in my mind: "Weeping may endure for a night, but joy cometh in the morning" (Psalm 30:5b). Because these psalms are so honest about the dried throat and the weeping, the horrible pit and the miry clay, I can trust that they are also honest about the new song and the joy that comes in the morning.

The biblical scholar Water Brueggemann writes about trusting these psalms as an act of "bold faith":

> The use of these "psalms of darkness" may be judged by the world to be *acts of unfaith and failure*, but for the trusting community,

their use is *an act of bold faith*, albeit a transformed faith. It is an act of bold faith on the one hand, because it insists that the world must be experienced as it really is and not in some pretended way. On the other hand, it is bold because it insists that all such experiences of disorder are a proper subject for discourse with God.[29]

In the depths of my depression, disorder overwhelmed my life. Through the psalms of lament, I found a way to bring this disorder to God. No denial, no pretending—I bring only the truth. I know so well how prone I am to doubts and questions. Yet in this act of honesty, I practice what Brueggemann calls "bold faith." By doing this, I open myself to hope, "the joy that comes in the morning." This does much to sustain my recovery. It leaves me with deep gratitude to the psalmists, who long ago had the courage and faith to bring their suffering to God. In this spirit, I offer the psalms to you.

HELP 29

Expressing Gratitude

As a young man, my father moved with his family from their farm in King and Queen County, Virginia, to Richmond, the state capital. Like so many others, the family had lost its farm during the Great Depression, and the move was an economic necessity. In spite of leaving home, my dad never lost his ties to King and Queen County. Over the years he'd frequently go back there to hunt and fish with relatives.

When I was eight or nine, I started going "down to the country" with my dad. He bought me a shotgun and a fishing rod, and he taught me how to use them. At home I always felt under pressure from my dad to make the best grades and get into the best college. But in the country, I never felt pressure from him to be the best shot or to catch the most fish. Maybe this was because he was comfortable being back home. He slowed down to country speed, and we just had a good time. He'd smoke his pipe and teach me the songs he loved. We went back to "The Red River Valley" every time we drove home from King and Queen. I owe my singing style—off-key, enthusiastic, and improvisational when I forget the words—to my dad.

I haven't gone hunting since my dad died, and I'm not much of a fisherman—especially for a Minnesotan. My life has taken me to other places, and my home today is far away from King and Queen County. But I still smile when I remember going down to the country. Some of the best things that ever happened to me as a child took place in King and Queen County.

One of my dad's cousins had a son close to my own age, and we soon became friends. He'd stay at our house in Richmond, and I'd stay on his folks' farm in King and Queen. When I was staying with him, most evenings after supper, while it was still light, his father would take me out in his car to go groundhog hunting. We'd drive the back roads, just about every road in that county was a back road, stop at a likely looking bean field, and scan the field for bare patches that might indicate where groundhogs had been feeding or where their holes were. If we saw a groundhog feeding in the beans or poke his head up out of the hole, I'd carefully raise my 22 magnum rifle with a low-power scope, take careful aim, and, if I was lucky, my friend's dad would soon be congratulating me on a good shot.

My takeaway from those years isn't from the hunting but from this man's kindness toward me. After working all day on his dairy farm, he could have relaxed at home in front of the TV. Instead, he took his son's city friend out looking for groundhogs. He was quiet, and I don't remember much talk beyond "Don't you see him over there by that big stump?" and "That's OK. You'll get the next one."

He died many years ago, the result of a farming accident. I miss him, and I wish I could tell him how much those hunting expeditions meant to me as a child. I'd like to thank him for what he taught me about kindness and generosity. Actually I probably did thank him at the time—I was brought up to say thank you—but I would have done that without thinking. Back then, I just assumed that taking city kids out hunting, city kids who often missed easy shots, was just something he did. Now I realize how much of a gift of time and care he was giving me. If I could say thank you to him now, he would know how much I meant it.

Gratitude finds its power when we move from saying thank you by rote to saying it from the heart. Recovery is so much about reconnecting with people, escaping the isolation of mental illness, and accepting the help that is offered to us. For such gifts, heartfelt gratitude is the only apt response. I would encourage you to never assume that others know how much you appreciate what they have done for you. Make sure they know that—for your sake as well as for theirs. I invite you to think about someone who has been for you as my friends' father was for me. Remember all that person did for you. Take time to savor it. Let the gratitude well up inside. Feel how it calms and heals. Then, if it's still possible, let the person know how grateful you are.

In *An Altar in the World*, the pastor and theologian Barbara Brown Taylor writes about gratitude and its impact upon how we treat ourselves and others: "To become fully human means learning to turn my gratitude for being alive into some concrete good. It means growing gentler toward human weakness."[30] This quotation amplifies gratitude beyond a response to the kindness of another person into a response for the gift of life itself.

During the worst times of my depression, I didn't feel much gratitude for being alive or for anything else. Now, at least most days, I am grateful for my life and grateful to the people who have helped bring joy back to me. In recovery I live with the feeling of having opened up to the world and the people around me, loving life even as I know how hard life can be. Since I know this, I believe I have become gentler toward others, more forgiving, less judgmental, and more willing to help. When I act to help others, doing what Brown Taylor calls "concrete good," I like to believe I'm also showing gratitude to a man who was good to me many years ago in King and Queen County, Virginia.

Help 30

Finding Help from Other Times

IN A MENTAL HEALTH crisis, when everything is urgent and right now, it feels like the present is the only time you have. In recovery, you learn to relax from the present. You find help in other times. The past can provide understanding and perspective; the future can open up possibilities and nurture hope. The following short pieces offer help from these other times.

THE PAST

Lessons learned from the history of the treatment of mental illness have helped me understand my own treatment, especially the striking differences between my first two psychiatrists.

My in-patient psychiatrist prescribed meds, but what he really liked to do was tell stories. He had stories about cars, frogs, greased pigs, old rubber bands, knights in shining armor, and gangsters with machine guns. In one story, I was like an old rubber band that had been stretched one too many times. In another, I was like a car that had been driven too fast and too far without an oil change. His point was that I needed to rest and to allow my brain's stock of neurotransmitters (like serotonin and norepinephrine) to replenish. He told me another story to point out that I was relying on outdated defense mechanisms (like denial) rather than learning new ways of coping. In doing this, I was like a knight who constantly shined his armor, as if that was going to protect him against gangsters armed with machine guns. In another story, he compared my racing thoughts to greased pigs slipping and tumbling over one another. In my recovery, he said that I was like a brave young frog who'd hopped out of the dark well to face the risks and challenges of living in a bright new world. While he told that story, he made little hopping motions with his hands. I'm not sure if he had learned the frog story in med school or in kindergarten.

My second psychiatrist, the one I saw immediately after my discharge from the hospital, was quite different, emphatically not the story-telling type. He always began our sessions with a back and forth about meds. With his computer in front of him, he went over what medications I was taking, asking questions and taking notes. Only then did he move on to a check-in about my mood and my progress in going back to work. To his credit, he listened carefully and affirmed where he could, but he never departed from specifics. If I'd told him that in recovery I was feeling more and more like a young frog, I don't think he'd have understood this as progress.

Once I begin to read more about the history of mental health care, I realized that these two professionals were living out an ancient division in this history. My first psychiatrist was akin to the school of Plato, who held that mental illness was a "disharmony of the soul," which could be treated by living according to the wisdom of philosophy. In this way one gains self-knowledge and a guide to life. Calling his stories "philosophy" seems a stretch, but for me they have, in fact, been an opening to self-knowledge and a guide in recovery.

My second psychiatrist, who always began with pills, was like the physician Hippocrates, who believed that mental illness had a physical cause, an imbalance in the four humors: blood, phlegm, black bile, and yellow bile. For him a depressive temperament was the result of an excess of black bile. Though Hippocrates's humoral theory has long since been disproved, his emphasis on the physical cause of mental illness was reflected every time my psychiatrist looked up from his computer and asked about my meds.

Many centuries have passed, but these two schools of thought endure, and we are fortunate that this is the case. I know my own recovery has benefited from both talk therapy and medication, the legacies of Plato and Hippocrates. Andrew Solomon writes, "Though the data in this field is complicated, it suggests that the combination of drugs and therapy works better than either one alone."[31] We owe a debt of gratitude to both of these ancient Greeks.

THE NEAR PRESENT

Cymbalta was approved as a treatment for major depression in 2004. When I was hospitalized a year or so later, my in-patient psychiatrist prescribed it for me, a prescription that showed he was actually a follower of Hippocrates as well as Plato. I stayed on this medication for almost ten years, until I gradually weaned myself off it under supervision. When my psychiatrist prescribed it, he told me it would "put a floor under my depression." It did just that. Unlike some other drugs I took in those years, it didn't seem to have any significant side effects, and I believe it played a major role in preventing my need for further hospitalizations. If I had been hospitalized a year or so earlier, this drug would not have been available. Maybe another drug would have worked as well, an effective drug on the first try, though I doubt it. I feel fortunate that Cymbalta was around when I needed it.

New drugs are always becoming available. If your current medication is not working, there is realistic hope that a new drug might work. A recent development may expedite the process of finding the right medication. A cotton swab is used to collect a DNA sample from inside one's cheek. Then the sample is tested to determine the likely effectiveness of a medication as well as possible side effects and the best dosage. If you've spent weeks trying out a drug only to find that it's unhelpful and then more weeks determining whether it's helpful at a higher dosage, this test could save time, pain, and anxiety.

Besides new medications, enhanced versions of old methods of treatment are becoming available. In the hospital, I met a young musician who was about to undergo ECT (electroconvulsive therapy). He was terrified of the damage it might do to his memory and his ability to perform. New developments in ECT therapy have allowed for the sharp reduction or the total elimination of such side effects. For those living with "treatment-resistant depression," when neither psychotherapy nor medication has offered relief from symptoms, ECT may be the best hope of recovery.

THE FUTURE

The future promises continuing development and refinement of new types of treatment and therapy. Magnetic seizure therapy (MST) uses a magnetic field to induce seizures in the cerebral cortex, with the intention of producing the benefits of ECT but without the electrical jolt to the part of the brain that impacts memory. Transcranial magnetic stimulation (TMS) employs a magnetic field to stimulate brain cells, causing a decrease in depressive symptoms. Vagus nerve stimulation (VNS) involves planting a pacemaker-like device in the chest, sending impulses along the vagus nerve to bring relief from symptoms. Deep brain stimulation (DBS), in which electrodes are implanted in the brain, has been proven effective in treating a variety of conditions, including Parkinson's disease, epilepsy, and obsessive-compulsive disorder; it is now in clinical trials as a treatment for depression.

I realize that my account of these therapies and treatments reflects my lack of knowledge. My point isn't to offer definitions and exact descriptions that are beyond my scientific understanding but to offer realistic hope. Even if nothing seems to be helping now, there may well be a treatment in the near future that will help.

BACK TO THE PAST

Dr. Samuel Johnson, the eighteenth-century master of multiple literary genres, is best known for his monumental work *A Dictionary of the English Language.* In addition to fame, Johnson knew "the black dog," his term for depression. He wrote, "When I rise my breakfast is solitary, the black dog waits to share it, from breakfast to dinner he continues barking."[32] Johnson found relief from his "black dog" by writing about it and through conversing with Samuel Boswell, his biographer, who also lived with depression.[33] As I write this book and as I talk about my depression with people I trust, I think of Dr. Johnson and thank him for helping to prepare the way.

Help 31

Not Being Alone

FOLLOWING ARE ACCOUNTS OF depression, or something like it, from three sources. The first is ancient and biblical; the second, from the nineteenth century, is political; and the third is nearly contemporary and intensely personal.

First, from Psalm 102 in the Bible, a lament from out of the depths:

> For my days are consumed like smoke, and my bones are burned as an hearth.
>
> My heart is smitten, and withered like grass; so that I forget to eat my bread.
>
> By reason of the voice of my groaning my bones cleave to my skin.
>
> I am like a pelican of the wilderness: I am like an owl of the desert.
>
> I watch, and am as a sparrow alone upon the house top. (Psalm 102:3–7)

Second, an account of a mental health crisis that Abraham Lincoln experienced as a young man, from the biography *Team of Rivals* by Doris Kearns Goodwin:

> The awkward dissolution of his engagement to Mary and the anticipated loss of his best friend combined with the collapse of the internal improvement projects and the consequent damage to his reputation to induce a state of mourning that deepened for weeks. He stopped attending the legislature and withdrew from the lively social life he had enjoyed. His friends worried that he was suicidal. According to Speed, "Lincoln went Crazy—had to remove razors from his room—take away all Knives and other such dangerous things—&c—it was terrible."[34]

Third, from an autobiography, *Darkness Visible*, by William Styron:

> I had now reached that phase of the disorder where all sense of
> hope had vanished, along with the idea of a futurity; my brain, in
> thrall to its outlaw hormones, had become less an organ of thought
> than an instrument registering, minute by minute, varying degrees
> of its own suffering.[35]

A psalm from the Bible, a biography of Abraham Lincoln and his political rivals, and an account by a famous author of his mental suffering—
these three quotations seem to have little in common. They do not overlap
in time or place, nor in genre or style. But in spite of their differences, each
speaks about depression and each tells us who live with this illness that we
are not alone.

If the words from the psalm are typed out on a clean sheet of paper
so there is no indication of where they come from, it would be easy to take
them as a contemporary poet's lament over her depression. There are many
psalms like this in the Bible, laments that could have been written by a sister of Anne Sexton or Sylvia Plath, great poets who struggled with mental
illness. Like Psalm 102, these psalms are clinically accurate in describing
the symptoms of depression: groaning, feeling flushed, loss of appetite, inability to sleep, feeling isolated and disoriented. These psalms were written
many centuries ago, yet I hear in them the reality of my own suffering.

Many have written about the connection between depression and loss.
The quotation from *Team of Rivals* details the losses that simultaneously
struck Lincoln: Joshua Speed, his best friend, was moving away; his engage-
ment to Mary Todd was on the rocks; his social life had disappeared; and
his political career seemed to have reached a dead end. Scholars debate
whether Lincoln was living with what today we would call major depression, but there is no denying that these losses took a terrible toll on his
mental health.

In my earlier book about my illness, *A Pelican of the Wilderness*, I
bring together various factors that I believe contributed much to my hospitalizations: the loss of companionship when our children moved away from
home, the loss of regular exercise because an injury prevented my daily
long-distance runs, the waning of self-respect as I convinced myself that I
was staying at my church solely for paychecks and regular vacations. There
is much in my own experience that draws me toward Lincoln or anyone
else who experiences a string of losses.

The quotation from *Darkness Visible* is breathtaking in its honesty and clinically precise in its catalog of pain—a 10+ on a scale of 1–10, when the brain functions only to register suffering in body, mind, and spirit. This could have been written about my time in the ER, a description truer to that experience than anything else I've ever read. Even in what was for me a singularly terrible time, someone else knew what it was like.

Others I quote in *Forty-Nine Helps*—Andrew Solomon, Deborah Serani, Kathleen Norris, Scott Stossel, Brené Brown, and Parker Palmer—are open about their own struggles with mental suffering. Like Styron, they have the courage and ability to write exact descriptions of internal pain. I want to learn whatever they can teach me from research and study, but it is their suffering—their openness about what they've lost and what they've learned—that draws me toward them.

Hearing the stories of others who have lived with depression or experienced a mental health crisis breaks through our isolation and diminishes our shame. Their stories teach us that even when mental illness takes us to the worst places, we are not alone.

Help 32

Getting Help

Georgia O'Keeffe painted her pictures of flowers many times larger than they are in real life. She explained, "So I thought I'll make them big like the huge buildings going up. People will be startled; they'll have to look at them."[36] I have a similar hope for a story I've told in various churches. It makes one point, and it makes the point so obviously there is no way to miss it. I include the story here because the point is the key one in recovery from mental illness.

Once upon a time, there was a town in the kingdom ruled by Burger King. People were happy there, and life was good. That is, life was good except for one day a year. On that day, Burger King and his entourage visited their town to demand that the people pledge their loyalty to him and then do something to prove it. As the day of the visit came closer, people got more and more anxious about what the king would ask of them this year.

The dreaded day finally came. At sunrise people gathered in the town square, all eyes on the road that the king would take from his castle. A young man climbed up a tall tree so he could see the first glint of sun off the king's crown as the king approached the town. Soon the young man was crying out, "The king is coming. The king is coming. Better get your act together." And all too soon Burger King and his knights of the Round Whopper Table were in the center of the town square.

At the king's arrival, the people bowed their heads and held their breath. What would the king command of them this year? They didn't give them long to wait.

"Are the people of this town loyal?" Burger King asked with a ketchup-y rasp.

"Oh, yes, King. You know that we are loyal," the people all cried back in unison.

"Awesome. Then will you do what I command?"

"Oh, yes, you got that right."

"All righty then. Bring her in, boys."

The king signaled his knights, and then a huge cart creaked into the square. "Lift her down. Careful now. Careful." Slowly and with great care, the knights did as he commanded. There, shining in the light of the early morning sun, glistening with ketchup and mustard, with pickles drooping over the edge, was a giant hamburger, the largest ever made.

Pointing to the great burger, the king said, "I've got some good news and some bad news. The good news is that this is a free burger. You don't even need a coupon. The bad news is that if you don't eat every bit of it by sundown, you'll be banished to the ketchup factory. And remember that you can never get ahead in the ketchup factory. You can only catch up. I'll be back when the sun goes down."

With that the king turned, gathered up his bad puns, and left town with his entourage. The people burst out in panic, "What are we going to do?"

"That burger's ginormous. Even if I hadn't eaten in a week, I couldn't even make a dent in it."

"You got that right. See that pickle. It's bigger than a garbage pail lid."

"It's bigger than one of Georgia O'Keeffe's flowers."

"We're doomed. No way will we ever meet the challenge of Burger King."

"We might as well put our houses on the market and head for the ketchup factory."

Then a young boy, the same spry fellow who'd climbed up the tree to keep a lookout for the king, shocked the crowd. "We're not doomed," he said. "We're just going to have an early lunch." With that, he walked up to the burger, which was now at the perfect eating temperature, pulled out his trusty pocket knife, sliced off a piece, and ate it. "Not bad," he said while wiping a dribble of ketchup from the edge of his mouth. "Someday there will be far better burgers. But this is OK for a fast-food lunch. Come on, everybody! Gather round and cut off a hunk. We can have this baby done before it gets cold and disgusting."

So that's just what they did. Everybody gathered around, and they started cutting off hunks. Instead of a disaster, they were having a party! It was so much fun that they started calling friends in neighboring villages on their primitive flip phones, and more and more people piled into the town square. Soon all that was left of the ginormous burger was a very large, very stained hamburger wrapper.

With the burger done and a well-deserved siesta taken, the people were eager for the king to come back and see their loyalty. And sure enough, right at sunset, they heard the clatter of the approaching horses' hoofs, and soon the king was back in the middle of the square. When he saw the empty wrapper, he smiled and asked, "Who was it that showed you how to meet the challenge of Burger King?" With confidence the boy stepped in front of the king, bowed perfunctorily and said, "I did, Your Majesty. When they thought about eating the ginormous burger alone, they felt defeated. I showed them that if we do it together, help each other out, then it's no problem at all."

The king responded, "Young man, you are wise beyond your years, just as I was as a youth. You will go far, but never to the ketchup factory. You have a profitable future in store for you. By the way, what is your name?"

"My name is Ronald McDonald. It is my destiny to meet the challenge of Burger King."

OK, not exactly a finalist for the international short-story contest, but this story does make its one point, and I hope makes it so big that, like one of O'Keeffe's flowers, you won't be able to miss it. Just like you can't eat a ginormous hamburger without help, you can't recover from mental illness without help either. That's the one point: *There is no recovery without help.* And as Ronald McDonald knew, once you ask for help, help is available. But you have to ask.

Help 33

Fighting Dragons and Overcoming Depression

SOMETIMES I COMPARE MY depression to a dragon. Like the way dragons are depicted in myth and legend, the worst times of my depression were terrifying, implacable, and beyond my understanding. Depression took over my life as completely as a dragon takes over whatever territory it wants.

Though terrifying and fearsome enemies, neither a dragon nor depression is omnipotent. The following stories offer two different ways of overcoming a dragon. We will find that they have marked similarities to two different ways of overcoming depression.

The story of St. George and the dragon is the more well-known of the two tales. In one version of the story, a fierce dragon is threatening a great city. When no other sacrifice will satisfy the dragon's wrath and hunger, the citizens start feeding it their own children. Whenever such a meal is due, the child to be sacrificed is chosen by lot. Finally the lot falls on the king's daughter, who is then left by a pond for the dragon to come and devour.

As good fortune would have it, St. George chances upon the spot where she is awaiting her death. She pleads for him to go away—she is brave and determined to sacrifice herself to save her city—but he refuses to abandon her. When the dragon appears, Saint George makes the sign of the cross, charges forward on horseback, and seriously wounds the dragon with his lance. The wound tames the beast, so he is able to lead it around on a leash.

St. Martha also overcame a dragon, but her technique was quite different. In a variant of this story, the dragon is the Tarasque, a fearsome beast made of the parts of several animals. It has a lion's head, a turtle's shell, six bearlike legs, and a tail that ends in a scorpion's stinger. The king and his knights had attacked the beast to stop it from devastating the countryside and terrorizing the people, but they were unable to defeat it. When St. Martha encounters the Tarasque, she does not attack it with lance or sword. Instead, by singing hymns and offering prayers, she gentles it into submission. This certainly takes more time and patience than a head-on charge with a lance, but it avoids bloodshed. In the end it achieves the same result: St. Martha overcomes the Tarasque, she secures it with a leash, and the beast follows wherever she leads.

As we see from these two legends, there is more than one way to overcome a dragon. The same is true with overcoming depression. Sometimes, like St. George, we need to come at depression head on, using whatever lance we have. I think of medications as a modern lance. The right one can have direct impact on depression, just as St. George's lance most surely had direct impact on the dragon. It won't end the depression, but just as St. George did with the dragon, the right meds will get the depression under control.

For me cognitive behavioral therapy (CBT) has been another trusty lance with direct impact in my struggle with depression. I learned the rudiments of CBT as part of a crisis management group when I was first hospitalized. CBT has helped me to attack my depression by showing how cognitive distortions—perfectionism, overgeneralization, catastrophizing, jumping to conclusions, and all the other types of illogical thinking that cause me pain—are integral to my illness. These cognitive distortions can be tough to reach with an ordinary lance—they make me think of a dragon covered with thick scales—but CBT is their equal. By exposing these distortions for what they are, toxic and dangerous, CBT has greatly diminished their power to do me harm.

Talk therapy has more in common with St. Martha's strategy of gentling the dragon into submission. It's not so much about making a direct impact on depression as slowly changing the conditions in which depression thrives. Letting go of the demands I place on myself, replacing denial with more effective ways of coping with life's demands, establishing clear boundaries to demarcate where my responsibility ends—these are all changes I have made through therapy and practice. I still have work to do, but over the years I have learned to follow the example of St. Martha and I have made good progress in gentling these dragons into submission.

As my recovery has continued, I have kept on this same path. The emphasis on getting help, the focus on pleasure in recovery, the encouragement to find sources of self-worth, the respect for one's own story, the recovery of humor, the honoring of one's freedom and agency, the maintenance of balance and perspective—so much in this book feels like St. Martha's approach to overcoming a dragon. Looking over the last fourteen years, I'd say that earlier in my recovery I needed the right meds and the insights of cognitive behavioral therapy, the recovery equivalent to St. George's stout lance and noble horse. Now it's more hymns and prayers, consolidating what I've learned over time and taking good care of myself. That isn't to say that there aren't still days when I need to grab my favorite lance and go at the beast head on.

HELP 34

Being, Doing, and Learning

TOWARD THE END OF the baseball movie *Bull Durham*, Crash Davis (Kevin Costner), a journeyman minor-league catcher, is cut from the Durham Bulls and assigned to a lower-level minor-league team in Asheville, North Carolina. You would think there's no way Crash, a savvy veteran, is going to accept the demotion. He's past his prime and his career is going in the wrong direction. Of course he knows it's time to quit and get on with his life after baseball. But instead of quitting, he packs his gear, loads up his car, and drives to Asheville.

It doesn't make any sense—until you see what happens. He plays in Asheville just long enough to hit a home run, number 247 of his minor-league career, and then he does quit. According to the movie, this homer makes him the all-time minor-league home run champion, the record holder. Even so, the game doesn't stop and no sky rockets are set off in honor of Crash's record-breaking home run. It's clear that he is the only one in the ball park who knows what it means.

No matter, Crash did it for himself, for his love of baseball, for the sheer pleasure of knocking the ball over the fence one last time. Number 247 gives him a place in baseball history, whether anybody else knows about it. There is so much recovery wisdom in Crash's behavior. In the process of setting the record, he claims self-worth and self-respect, while pursuing a goal that is deeply meaningful for him. He acts as an agent, making his own decisions on the basis of what is important to him. He accepts reality, but he doesn't let reality prevent him from finding pleasure in life. Both for playing baseball and for recovering from mental illness, this is healthy behavior.

He isn't the only character in the movie who has lessons to teach us. There's also Annie (Susan Sarandon), the muse for the Durham Bulls, who quotes Walt Whitman and teaches a fire-balling rookie pitcher the importance of breathing through his eyelids while pitching. She knows that wearing a garter belt can be the perfect remedy for a pitcher in a slump. She is also the only person in the movie besides Crash who knows what the minor-league home run record is. Actually, Annie says she knew the moment Crash broke it, even though he's in Asheville and she's in Durham. She's a master of nonlinear quantum reasoning.

OK, Annie may be a little quirky around the edges, but she's also brave and she doesn't hide from painful realities. She sums up life for people like Crash and herself: "The world is made for people who aren't cursed with self-awareness."[37] For such people life is easy—no troubling second thoughts or frustrating what-ifs. But Annie and Crash aren't like this. They are self-aware, and they are hurting because of it. They know they are not where they hoped to be in their lives. Crash is not going back to the majors, and Annie is going nowhere with her current pitcher boyfriend, who has lots of raw talent but no self-awareness whatsoever.

Annie is one of my favorite film characters. I love her honesty and intelligence and her total courage of her convictions. But is she right when she describes self-awareness as a curse? I know there is a kind of hypercritical self-awareness that gives one no peace; it is indeed a curse. In my depression, I constantly reviewed, examined, and then re-examined my every thought and deed. I could not stop judging myself or stop worrying about how others were judging me. It's the kind of exhausting, constant self-awareness that prompted the poet Sylvia Plath to cry out, "Is there no way out of the mind?"[38] That is indeed a curse.

But there is another kind of self-awareness that yields self-knowledge; it is a blessing. It's this kind of self-awareness that allows Annie to see that her life is stuck. In therapy, it's what allows us to recognize illogical ways of thinking and self-defeating patterns of behavior that contribute to our depression. Such awareness is essential to escape from our minds and to find a fulfilling life in the real world. As *Bull Durham* comes to an end, Annie has the opportunity to do just this.

On a rainy afternoon, Annie finds Crash sitting alone in the swing on her front porch. He tells her he's quit playing baseball, and she tells him she's quit the fastball pitcher. Crash says there's a possibility of his getting a job as manager of a team in Visalia next year. Could he make it back to the major leagues as a manager? She is quick to say that he can, telling him about how he could be a great manager because baseball is a nonlinear, spacious thing. She is just getting started when he stops her.

> Crash: Annie, I got a lot of time to hear your theories, and I want to hear every damn one of them. But, now I'm tired and I just . . . don't want to think about baseball. And I don't want to think about quantum physics. And I don't want to think about nothing. I just . . . I just want to be.
>
> Annie: I can do that too.[39]

This is a chance for Annie to change her life. Unlike the fastball pitcher, Crash values her as an equal, a partner in facing what might come next in life. Though she's ready to leave Durham and make a new life with Crash, she's not just going to be a tag along as he pursues a job as a manager. Whatever happens will be a joint enterprise. They both have too much self-respect and self-esteem for it to be any other way.

"I just want to be." "I can do that too." What a great way to end a movie! Maybe they're not there yet, but Crash and Annie are moving toward self-acceptance, to a place where they can simply be at peace for a time. When plagued by self-criticism and unrelenting high expectations, just being was not possible for me. I could not even just be asleep; I had to stay awake to review my failures and to anticipate the new pain tomorrow would bring. I can still get stressed out and worn down, but now I have people to talk with and hard-won skills on how to put things back into perspective. My self-esteem is no longer contingent on my latest accomplishment. If I just want to be, I can do that too.

HELP 35

Receiving Unexpected Gifts of Kindness

My first night on the psych unit someone said to me, "Do not worry, sir. You will soon be home." These encouraging words were all the kinder for being spoken in a gentle lilting voice. The speaker wasn't a doctor nor a member of the hospital's therapeutic staff, but a housekeeper. She was a beautiful Somali woman with an orange scarf and a long purple dress. A few minutes earlier, she had knocked gently on the door of my room and actually waited until I said, "Come in." A small thing, but she was the only one to wait. All the other hospital staff had knocked and entered without taking time for me to respond. I never saw her again, but I have not forgotten her kindness, a quiet gift at a desperate time.

This was one of many unexpected gifts that have nourished my recovery. I think of the elderly woman on the psych unit with her gifts of mixed nuts and recovery wisdom. I think of the psychiatrist on the psych unit who told me he was treating me as a peer. I think of a friend who sent us a meal in a box as a get-well gift the first time I was discharged. I think of another friend who volunteered to preach for me my first Sunday home. I accepted her offer at the last minute, and a crisis was averted. I think of a friend who sent me a card. I received so many cards for which I am grateful, but this friend wrote on it that he'd been saving this card for years until the right person needed it. I think of my son who came over at night from law school to sit with dad while trying to do a little bit of homework.

My church held a party to honor my long service. There I received many gifts: more cards, a check, a memory scrapbook, and some great lemon bars. The event itself was a gift, a chance to say goodbye with dignity to people I had served for more than twenty-five years. We shared so many wonderful stories, and I heard again and again that I had made someone's life better. It helped me to reclaim some of the good I had done in that place, a process that has continued throughout my recovery. It's hard to feel ashamed of the work that you've done when people are telling you they could not have made it through a difficult time if you had not been there for them.

Toward the end of the event, a young man in the congregation who knew a lot about mental pain from his own experience gave me the gift of hard-earned wisdom. Over lemon bars, he said, "Don't forget to brush your own teeth." I did wonder for a passing moment whether this was a caution about dental hygiene, but, of course, it wasn't. I don't know whether it was something that he had learned in a support group, heard from a therapist, or coined himself. I do know that it's shorthand for core recovery wisdom: stay rooted in the real world, respect your body, do the things that are necessary, and don't get lost in your head. Some people use post-it notes to put their favorite saying on the refrigerator or on the bathroom mirror. Others go a step further and have the words tattooed on their arms or some other body parts. I don't have to do any of that. Every time I brush my teeth, I remember what the young man said.

Recently at Vail Place, a member told me he was grateful I was there because my presence made him feel calmer. I was surprised and deeply gratified. I know this member well, and he is not the kind of person who's free with compliments, far from it. When he said he was grateful to me, it was from the heart, and I knew I had been given a gift. Spending time at Vail Place is an important part of my recovery, and he had affirmed that my decision to participate in the community there made a difference in his life. There's something wonderful in thinking that I, who had once melted down with stress, could now help somebody feel calm. If I need clear evidence that my recovery is flourishing, this is it!

From these and many other experiences, I have learned that affirmation, kindness, and wisdom can come from anybody, no professional title required. Nothing against the professionals; I owe them a lot. But with a therapist you always wonder whether their affirmation and positive feedback are the real deal or simply what they've learned to say as helping professionals. With my friend at Vail Place, I knew the affirmation was the real deal.

With most gifts, I have learned to simply say thank you and to enjoy them, but I still struggle to accept the gifts that I feel are unearned. For example, when people tell me how much they value my honesty in talking about my illness and thank me for my openness, I feel a little like a fraud.

The truth is that this honesty now comes easily to me, and I feel that I don't deserve their gratitude. Should I tell them they don't need to thank me for something that requires little effort on my part?

But the more I've thought about this, the more I am inclined to say nothing and just enjoy their gratitude. After all, if I had been born with perfect pitch and could out sing a nightingale (demonstrably not the case), people would compliment me on my voice. I'm sure that would make me feel good, even though perfect pitch took no effort on my part. For whatever reason, now I can talk honestly about my depression and people compliment and thank me. I'm doing my best to accept the gift they are giving me and not to discount this kindness.

Besides, failing to enjoy a sincere compliment feels a lot like taking your eye off pleasure, and a wise woman on the psych unit once warned me against doing that. I have received so many gifts in recovery—kindness, wisdom, affirmation. To adapt liturgical language, I feed on them in my heart.

Help 36

Giving Unexpected Gifts of Kindness

HAVING RECEIVED SO MANY gifts myself, I try to be generous with others. For example, I always leave a $5 bill in a conspicuous place when I check out of a hotel room. When I leave the cash, I imagine the pleasure it's going to give the person who comes in to clean the room after I check out. Five dollars isn't going to pay the bills, but it does say thank you. It does say that I recognize you exist and that I'd like to make your day a little better.

Is making someone feel better all there is to it, or do I leave the $5 mostly to make myself feel good? And, even if there was some real altruism in putting down the $5 at the time, am I spoiling whatever good I did by writing about my generosity? These questions remind me of how I used to rummage around in my motives until I convinced myself that whatever I had done, I had acted out of selfishness or for some other negative reason. Now I just accept that my motives are beyond sorting out and that whatever I do, I do for mixed motives—the chaff right there along with the wheat. I simply believe that the $5 brightens someone's day, and I know that doing it makes me feel good. Two goods by my count and no bads. I'm going to keep doing it, maybe even pop for $10 when I stay for more than one night.

At Vail Place we sign lots of birthday and get-well cards. Often there's a clipboard with a bunch of cards lying on the table in the living room. Anybody who wants can sign the cards. When I signed a group of cards recently, I had to look for an open space where I could put my name. OK, it's not a big deal, but I bet a card covered with signatures means more than a card with only a few signatures, and I've just increased the coverage. If I can write a little note, all the better. I add a little to someone's pleasure when that person receives the card, and I feel good about doing it. Again, two goods by my count and no bads.

I believe that recovery is enhanced by doing seemingly small things for others. Besides, how do we know if our deed is small? That $5 or even that signature could have been really important, coming at just the right time. A thank you may seem like another small thing, but there are times in my recovery when a thank you has made all the difference, and I haven't forgotten it. Small kindnesses do matter.

Somebody let me in front of her in the check-out line—I had one carton of milk; she had a cart full of all the weekly specials—and suddenly my day turned from dreary to not all that bad. A neighbor baked extra rhubarb bars and brought us over a plateful. Another neighbor kept going with his snowblower and did our sidewalk. A dreary day, made far worse by snow in April, turned into a day that was not all that bad. (We Minnesotans tend to understate, so "not all that bad" can be a celebration for us.)

These seemingly small things are the "random acts of kindness" that a once-popular bumper sticker encouraged us to practice. Opportunities to practice acts of kindness are all around us. I was trying to make coffee for the snack bar at Vail Place, but operating the new coffee maker was beyond me. A member—different race, different gender, and half my age—saw I was struggling and came over to help. She had the perfect teaching style to connect with somebody like me. Instead of giving in to impatience and making the coffee for me, she explained what I didn't understand without a hint of condescension and then patiently waited for me to work the machine. I'm now an expert on the coffee maker! I don't know what her motives were—I don't do motives anymore—I just know she made my day.

Following her example, I try to do the same for others, teaching them the tasks that I know how to do. Like the young woman who taught me to decode the mysteries of the new coffee maker, I try to do this respectfully and effectively. I always feel especially good when I train somebody to use the coffee maker.

There are many small ways that we can give kindness to others. I've mentioned the power of saying thank you. Here are some other small kindnesses that can make a difference. Catch the eye of someone and simply smile. I try to do this for new members at Vail Place when they are being welcomed at their first meeting. My smile adds to the welcome and helps them feel more comfortable among strangers. Do your best to remember people's names. This may seem obvious, but when people take the trouble to remember my name and use it when speaking to me, I feel special. I'm not that good with remembering names myself, so I have to work at it. Applaud for somebody. At Vail Place we often clap for the people who prepare a meal. I'm not a chef, but if I've cut up veggies for lunch, I feel some of the credit when people clap. Invite people so they feel included. For example, after lunch one day, somebody asked me to stay and compete in the red-hot chili-pepper eating contest. Absolutely no way! But it was so nice to be asked.

There's something else that's important in recovery about small acts of kindness. Mental illness tells us that we're useless; in fact, it tells us we're a liability. Doing even the seemingly smallest thing for somebody else shows this is a lie. I'm signing this card, talking to this guy, showing a new member how to make coffee. I'm going to be the one who starts the clapping at lunchtime. And as soon as Ingrid gets here, I'm going to ask her about the visit to her cousin in North Snowfield. Far from useless, I'm having an impact all over the place.

In a graduation address at Syracuse University that went viral, Professor George Saunders told the audience, "What I regret most in my life are failures of kindness."[40] When I think of regrets in my own life—something I don't do all that much anymore—I think first of major negative events, many of which cluster around my hospitalizations. But as I move deeper into recovery and think about what I regret today, I'm inclined to agree with Professor Saunders. In the future, I'm going to be careful not to let opportunities for showing kindness slip past me.

I'm vigilant for kindness. I leave no card in the pile unsigned. I try not to miss an opportunity to speak to people and use their names or to applaud at a meal, whether I cut up the vegetables or not. And I've about convinced myself to leave $10 if the motel stay was for more than one night. Would I do more than $10 for even longer stays? I'm not quite there yet in my recovery, but I'm moving in that direction.

HELP 37

Accepting Anger

IT SEEMED LIKE A good idea at the time. I took a community education class on how to make better use my android smartphone. I had bought the phone some months earlier because I'd taken a job at a church where texting was the primary means of communication with many of the members. I had a flip phone that could do texting, but it was slow and I didn't like to use it in public places. I had phone shame, so I bought the smartphone, did quite a bit of texting, and after some months became curious about other things my phone might do, things I often had seen other people do with great confidence and assurance. I suspect this means I had phone jealousy as well as phone shame! The class would easily solve all these problems, or so I thought.

Sue was also interested in the class, so on a snowy January morning we drove there together. Early in the class, the teacher suggested we take off whatever kind of protector we had on our phones so we could look at the back of the phone to see what was there. It sounded like a good idea to me, a bold journey into the unknown.

How wrong I was! I touched or loosened the wrong thing—I still don't know what—and a grisly icon appeared on the screen with the disquieting message "Erasing all data." I frantically raised my hand. When the teacher came over, I saw the look on her face that I've seen on church council members when they got their first glimpse of the next year's budget. By the time the icon disappeared, my phone was as lifeless as the Dead Sea.

For the next hour or so, I got to sit there with a cold phone and hot anger. I glared alternately at the dead phone and then at the teacher who had done me wrong. It was totally her fault. She had led me into the smartphone wilderness and left me there. I couldn't wait to get out of the class. Walking back to our car, which of course was now covered with ice and snow, I told Sue that I was absolutely never going back to that hideous class again. Later that afternoon, I started punching keys on my smartphone, using my trial-and-error skills. Suddenly "Restore data" popped up, and I was back in the smartphone business. The next two classes were excellent. By the end of the last class, I was using my phone as smoothly as a typical six-year-old.

Irritation is a symptom of depression. My phone's near-death experience brought me back to the way I felt when my depression was full-blown. Though I couldn't see it at the time, friends tell me now that I had become increasingly thin-skinned before my first hospitalization and that the least little thing would set me off. I didn't show full-blown anger or rage—I reserved that for myself—but I was so prickly, so easily irritated. Thankfully, the irritation I felt when my phone died was not a return to those days; it was just a reminder. Things like smartphones and smart TVs—things I want to master intuitively without effort—will probably always irritate me, but the irritation doesn't last, and it isn't the forerunner of an episode of depression.

Anger is another matter. I think of anger as irritation's big brother. I am trying to work out the role, if any, of anger in recovery. I have never been good at anger. Growing up, my father's powerful anger terrified me. He didn't get angry a lot, never physically lashing out at any of us. But when he did get angry, I wanted to run and hide. Early in life I learned to avoid anything that might set him off. In school, if somebody picked on me or tried to provoke a fight, I learned to turn the other cheek. I didn't do this because I was a good person. I did it because I didn't want to get into trouble and provoke my dad's anger.

These childhood lessons have caused me to fear anger and to keep it bottled up inside. But they haven't stopped me from feeling angry. If I think someone is laughing at me, making fun of something I've said or done, I feel a surge of anger. I also feel anger when I'm on the phone trying to clarify my cable-TV bill and end up feeling like I'm trying to get a firm grip on a handful of Jell-O. Likewise, some politicians simply piss me off.

One experience in particular has helped me see that in recovery there is more I want to do with anger than stuff it. On the psych unit, I kept a notebook where I journaled what happened to me every day. Journaling made me feel free of the unit for a time and gave me something I could control. Because the metal spiral binding of my notebook was deemed a potential instrument for self-harm, my notebook was kept at the nurses' station. Once when I went to ask for my notebook, the aide behind the desk made me wait for what felt like a long time and then told me she didn't know who I was. I believed she was trying to humiliate me, and I felt a flash of strong anger. I so wish that I had acted on my anger by telling her how I felt, not raging as my dad might have done, but being straightforward with my anger. Indeed, I did get some revenge, though indirectly. When I was finished journaling, I hid the notebook in my room and never had to ask anybody for it again.

I know letting some of my anger out would have been healthy and appropriate. Likewise, as I look back, I believe it would have been a good thing if I had told parishioners who I thought were being unfair and too demanding (there were never many of them, but there were always a few) that what they were doing was making me angry. Not in a rage, not out of control—I just would have liked to have told them honestly and without hesitation how I was feeling and why. I believe that would have helped me, but I never did it.

In recovery I'm working on expressing appropriate anger. I believe this is a matter of self-respect, an assertion that I will stand up for myself and that I believe in my own value. I'm working on expressing my anger in a way that's clear and forthright, not frightening like my dad's, and I'm feeling my way along. I want to use my anger to tell that cable-TV guy clearly and crisply what I think. I want to use it as motivation for political action. When you see me coming, you don't have to watch out. I'm not my dad. But if you treat me badly, piss me off, try to humiliate me like that aide did, you'll end up knowing exactly how I feel.

HELP 38

Looking into the Face of Beauty

IN 2001 WE FLEW to New York City to visit our younger son, who was then a student at New York University. As it turned out, we had scheduled one of the first flights out of Minneapolis after planes started flying again in the wake of 9/11. We wandered a Manhattan covered with posters pleading for information about loved ones who had disappeared in the destruction of the Twin Towers. At every police and fire station, we came across impromptu memorials of flowers and keepsakes for those who had given their lives trying to save the lives of others.

In the midst of all this, I read an article in *The New York Times* by Dr. Pauline Boss, who is known for her pioneering work on the theory of ambiguous loss.[41] It was not hard to see the 9/11 posters as the beginning of many people's journey into the world of ambiguous loss, a place where they sought a loved one who would never be found. For many more people who did not lose a loved one, there was the loss of the city they had known and the safety they had come to take for granted.

The New York Times quotes Dr. Boss as saying, "People must look into the face of beauty because they've seen the face of evil."[42] This may seem at first like an odd recommendation, but in New York at that time it offered a way forward. The evil was overwhelming, and ordinary life had ended. How could New Yorkers begin the task of adjusting to life in a new, terribly fraught reality? For Dr. Boss, the answer was beauty: confronted with the worst, she calls upon us to seek the best. Beauty can help free minds that had been paralyzed by an act of evil and its terrible consequences.

We followed her suggestion while we were in New York; we looked for beauty. We walked for hours in Central Park; we went to the Museum

118

of Modern Art and the Metropolitan Museum of Art; we went to a Broadway play. In some folder somewhere I still have the playbill signed by Ian McKellen, one of my favorite actors, who was hanging out at the stage door after the play.

We came home; though it took time, we settled back into our lives. For me this was not a good time, and as the months passed, my mood darkened. I reached a crisis point when depression took over my life. It was a face of evil that almost destroyed me. In recovery I have remembered the words of Dr. Boss and have sought the face of beauty.

I can frame my recovery as the return of beauty. In the first months of my recovery, I spent a lot of time at home alone. I usually had the radio on to classical music, background for whatever I was doing. I wasn't really listening, but it kept me company. Then there came a moment when background switched to foreground. The music wasn't just on; I was listening to it. Mozart grew louder than my self-accusative thoughts. I stopped ruminating and started listening, a personal triumph of beauty over evil. I began to see that how I listened to a piece of music was a measure of how much depression was intruding into my life. Most days now I can listen without some negative thought getting in the way. I smile when I think of it: my recovery is set to music!

There's synergy between looking into the face of beauty and recovery from mental illness. Once music captures one's attention, it doesn't want to let go. When I really listen to music, I relax, breathe more deeply, and simply calm down. Relaxed and calmer, I am even more able to keep the music in the foreground. There's nothing to worry about, and the music is so beautiful.

Beauty abounds. Seeking beauty, I have become an inveterate sunset watcher. This is a way I regularly look into the face of beauty and experience just how it is that beauty heals. Sunsets draw me out of myself, away from all my self-concerns, into mystery and wonder, so when I return home to myself, I am restored by the time away. And, of course, sunsets are only one of many ways we can find beauty in creation. Bright sun on fresh snow, sky so blue it dazzles—a winter day in Minnesota offers so much beauty. I remember summer evenings growing up in Virginia when the lightning bugs seemed to dance to the rhythm of the crickets. Wherever you live and whatever season you're in, nature invites you into beauty.

I seek beauty wherever I can find it. I'm reading a book and suddenly I come across something so perfectly written, so unique and right, that its beauty holds all my attention. I've had this same experience looking at a painting or a photograph that merges beauty with truth. Far from art and literature, I also find beauty when I watch a basketball player soar above the rim with grace and ease that takes my breath away. Right now, I'm learning to find beauty at the dining table, to enjoy a good meal as a work of art—something to be savored, not rushed through.

I have friends who are infatuated by the beauty of a well-designed sports car. For others it's an elegant computer program or the complexities of a smartphone. Yes, they're machines, but for people who can appreciate these machines, they are creations of great and intricate beauty. The world of handicrafts, from knitting needles to table saws, brings beauty into the lives of many. Some find beauty in the poses of yoga or the movements of dance. Others find it in the clothes they wear, turning themselves into objects of art. I invite you to add your own experiences of finding the face of beauty. Beauty really does abound.

Whenever evil touches our lives, as a society or as individuals, I believe Dr. Boss is right in urging us to seek the face of beauty. Accepting reality means not underestimating the power of evil to bring hurt. It also means not underestimating the power of beauty to bring healing.

HELP 39

Living in Balance and Harmony

THE LATE AUTHOR TONY Hillerman wrote wonderful mystery novels set on the huge Navajo reservation in the southwest. His writing takes you there, so you become intimate with barren landscapes and moments of spectacular beauty. At one with the land, you learn to rejoice when the rain finally comes. Adding to the richness of his novels, Hillerman weaves Navajo religion and culture into them so skillfully that you don't notice how much you're learning as you turn the pages while absorbed in the story.

What the Navajo call *hozro* is one of those things you learn about while reading Hillerman's stories. To have *hozro* means you are in harmony with what surrounds you so you are able to "live in beauty."[43] To me it means keeping my life in balance, not letting things get out of proportion. The loss of *hozro* is a serious matter; a Navajo healing ceremony may be required to restore a person to harmony.

Hozro seems like the Navajo word for "mental health." Indeed, there was a time when mental illness was described as being "un-balanced" and having a "dis-order." When my depression raged, I lost mental balance. Nothing I did was on the positive side of the judgment scale; everything weighed on the negative. My mind was profoundly out of balance. I desperately needed my own culture's version of a Navajo healing ceremony to restore my life to harmony so I might yet again "live in beauty."

In "On Self-Respect," an essay in her book *Slouching Towards Bethlehem,* Joan Didion describes what it is like when one's life is out of balance.

> Every encounter demands too much, tears the nerves, drains the will, and the specter of something as small as an unanswered letter

arouses such disproportionate guilt that answering it becomes out of the question. To assign unanswered letters their proper weight, to free us from the expectations of others, to give us back to ourselves—there lies the great, the singular power of self-respect.[44]

I have lived what Didion describes, lying awake at night in anguish because I had forgotten to return a phone call. This happened more than once, but I remember one particular night. I had failed to return a call to a leader in my church. I had probably blocked the call out of my mind because I was afraid he might say something that would increase my anxiety and make sleep even more impossible. By the time I remembered his call, it was too late to return it. My incompetence, my inability to do anything right, blazed up in my mind. I hated myself.

I lay awake imagining how my caller had waited by the phone for hours expecting me to get back to him, how furious he had become, and how he would retaliate by getting up a petition to have me fired. All night long my mind raced from one negative thought to another until I'd transformed my life into a horror show with worse yet to come. I started obsessing about suicide. I wanted to kill myself because of an unanswered phone call! This sounds incredible to me now, but that night it was my reality. Instead of giving his call its proper weight, I gave it so much weight that it almost crushed the life out of me.

For Didion, self-respect is the antidote for this kind of disproportionate fear and guilt. I understand self-respect as the very foundation of living in harmony with other people. I value myself, and I respect myself; I seek to do the same with others. Whatever enhances self-respect also enhances our ability to assign the proper weight to our obligations to other people. And that enhances our ability to live in harmony with others.

Achieving this goal can be assisted by cognitive behavioral therapy (CBT). CBT helps by pointing out the illogic that accompanies unbalanced thinking. In the case of my not returning the church leader's phone call, my thinking was distorted by what David Burns calls "magnification." He describes this kind of illogical thinking: "Magnification commonly occurs when you look at your own errors, fears, or imperfections and exaggerate their importance."[45] This is exactly what I had done on that awful night. Knowing that this kind of thinking, by which I terrorized myself, is illogical and distorted helps me free myself from it.

CBT brings reality to bear on how one thinks and feels. In reality it is a good thing to return phone calls—as well as letters, e-mails, texts, and other ever-multiplying electronic communications, though probably not notes in a bottle—and it is a good thing not to put off replying too long. But, at least in most cases (and never for a message in a bottle) you don't have to respond right this minute, creating a crisis where there isn't one, giving the response more weight than it requires.

Life happens, and we lose our way from time to time. Even our heartfelt desire to "live in beauty" and to maintain *hozro* can be overwhelmed by a health crisis, the loss of a job, family trouble, or some other major life disruption. The Navajo have known this for untold generations. They offer healing ceremonies for those who had lost the path of beauty. They give hope that balance once lost can be restored.

For most of us, there are no similar ceremonies, but there is still good hope that lost harmony can be regained. Didion and Burns offer us guidance in how to do this. Beyond their help, there is so much we learn in recovery that helps us to find balance in our minds and in our lives. To have this balance, to "live in beauty," is to have mental health.

HELP 40

Venting

IN RECOVERY I SEEK to live in beauty every day, preserving the balance and harmony of my life. Though it sounds counterintuitive, I've learned that to preserve balance I also need to erupt, blow off steam, and vent emotion—not every day, maybe not for weeks at a time, but absolutely every once in a while.

My first experience of doing this was on the psych unit. One night many of us gathered in front of the TV in the lounge to watch *Independence Day*, the movie where the president doesn't have all the facts about what's in Area 51, Roswell, New Mexico. I remember sitting on a sofa with a couple of other patients, munching popcorn, cheering loudly, and punching my fist into the air.

And why not? After some rough going, we humans were blowing the extraterrestrial invaders away. Not many of us sitting there had had much recent experience of being on the winning side of anything. Now we were winning the war of the worlds! The movie felt like just what we needed at the moment, not therapy or pills, but whumping on a bunch of space monsters.

I suspect that for many of us these monsters were more than just a bunch of ectoplasmic invaders. When we cheered as our side zapped the monsters, our cheering was fueled in part by our identifying them with all the frustrations and losses our illnesses had caused us. Watching the movie was a safe place to vent how we felt about all of this. No, we couldn't zap our illnesses, but we could be one with Captain Steve Hiller (Will Smith), a star in the movie, as he zapped with a vengeance—and that felt really good. It was a kind of vicarious getting even, a step toward feeling less helpless in the face of mental illness. We won! I suspect many of us slept better that night because we'd had a chance to let our feelings out. I know I did.

I practice a similar kind of zapping in reading the psalms from the Bible. No human emotion is taboo for the psalms, and this includes anger at the "enemies" who are responsible for some ill or suffering besetting the psalmist. Psalm 59 is one of the psalms that expresses such anger and seeks God's help against enemies. Verse 1 (NRSV) begins, "Deliver me from my enemies, O my God;" and then the psalm continues:

> For the sin of their mouths, the words of their lips,
> let them be trapped in their pride.
> For the cursing and lies that they utter,
> consume them in wrath;
> consume them until they are no more.
> Then it will be known to the ends of the earth
> that God rules over Jacob.
> Each evening they come back,
> howling like dogs
> and prowling about the city.
> They roam about for food,
> and growl if they do not get their fill. (Psalm 59:12–15, NRSV)

The psalmist is not specific about who the "enemies" are. None of the psalms dealing with enemies are specific; this allows them to be universal and timeless. As I did with the space monsters in *Independence Day*, I can identify these enemies with depression and its grisly minions, the cause of so much suffering in my own life. The psalm allows me to vent my anger and frustration against them. With no guilt, I can enthusiastically call upon God to consume my enemies in holy wrath, to obliterate them so they are no more.

In some psalms this call for divine zapping ends the matter, but in Psalm 59 there is a refrain in which the enemies keep returning like hungry dogs seeking to fill their bellies. At this point, I completely identify the dogs with my illness. Exactly like my depression, these dogs are insatiable, always wanting more pain, never satisfied with the amount of life they have chewed up. They can be stopped for a time, but they never run away. Each day I must be ready to face them yet again. Reading these psalms, I vent my anger and my frustration, acknowledge the ongoing struggle, and ask for God's help in facing these enemies.

Like watching the movie on the psych unit, reading these psalms is a safe way to vent pent-up feelings. Writing is another way. I felt so much better after sharing the following with a writing group at Vail Place.

> I'd feed my depression the liver they served at the Hillsborough County, New Hampshire, Nursing Home, where I was chaplain in the late 70s. Not to be ungrateful for a free lunch, but it was truly disgusting, tough and suspect. I'd give my depression a huge serving—eat until you gag on it—and then I'd give it some more. How about some Ovaltine? I hate Ovaltine. Want a side of cold, burned Brussel sprouts? And for dessert, here's some more yummy liver. Eat until you puke up your guts.

I encourage you to take a stab at writing a tirade against your own depression. You don't need to show it to anybody. Say exactly how you feel; let yourself rage. Virginia Woolf wrote, "Take notes and the pain goes away."[46] Letting feelings erupt in a piece of writing has done exactly this for me.

In *Acedia & Me*, Kathleen Norris describes an argument with her husband, David.

> Slamming a kitchen cupboard shut and sputtering with rage, I wanted to tell David that I hated him, though I knew that wasn't true. So I shouted, *"I don't like you very much!"* This broke us up, a laugh-until-you-cry gut-buster, and defused the tension.[47]

The argument between Kathleen Norris and her husband ends in a kind of mutual venting and emotional catharsis that reaffirmed their relationship. I used the same line while having an argument with my own spouse, and it broke us up and defused the tension. By now all we need to say is "Kathleen Norris," and we find it hard to stay mad at each other. At times the depression I live with has added much stress to our life together. When we can vent together, our bond is reaffirmed, and I know that I am not alone in facing my illness. I invite you to try Kathleen Norris's line the next time you are in an argument with a loved one.

I go back to that night watching *Independence Day* on the psych unit. I had so much fun venting feelings and vicariously zapping invading monsters. I felt such a bond with the other patients who enjoyed the movie with me. I hope that they are doing well in recovery.

HELP 41

Giving Help

UNLIKE ALL THE OTHER Helps with their focus on people living with depression, this one is focused on primary support persons and others who are committed to helping us.

HELP BY SHOWING UP

I quoted earlier from Doris Kearns Goodwin's book *Team of Rivals*, which provides a compelling account of a time early in President Lincoln's life when he underwent a mental health crisis. During the worst of it, his primary support was Joshua Speed, his best friend. Goodwin writes, "Throughout the nadir of Lincoln's depression, Speed stayed at his friend's side."[48]

My wife Susan was my Joshua Speed. When I was on the psych unit, I desperately needed the reassurance of her being there each day, and she was. Remembering those times, I do not know how I would have gotten through my hospitalization without her support. In the weeks and months of recovery that followed, other people helped, but she was still the person I counted on.

I know from my experience of ministry that being present with someone who is in pain can be difficult. I've said some of my most fervent prayers just before stepping into a hospital room, praying and hoping that the right words would come to me. I needed to do this to prepare myself. But the truth is that just by walking into the room, even before I said a word, I had already done much to help. In *What to Do When Someone You Love Is Depressed*, Mitch and Susan Golant write:

The fear of abandonment is endemic to the human condition, but it is also a large part of the black cloud that hovers over a depressed individual—especially if she has experienced a real abandonment.[49]

The fear of abandonment is allayed only by the presence of someone who cares. Being the primary support person is often very hard. If you are doing this for someone, then you are giving that person a vital gift. I have a couple of suggestions as to how you can make your support more effective, but I first want to emphasize that you are already doing the most important thing simply by being present.

My first suggestion is that you learn more about your loved one's illness, be it depression or something else. A class from the National Alliance on Mental Illness (NAMI) would be a good place to start. You can find a list of online classes at www.nami.org. Knowing more about mental illness will ease some of your own anxiety, as well as make you a more effective participant in your loved one's recovery. I would add that if you are feeling in need of support yourself, NAMI offers many types of support groups for caregivers and families of people living with mental illness.

My other suggestion—it's actually more urgent than a suggestion—is that you make time to take care for yourself. As my primary support person, in it for the long haul, Susan knew that it was essential to my recovery that she stay physically and mentally healthy. She paced herself, took breaks when needed, and stayed in touch with her own support system. Though my care absorbed a lot of her time, Susan still tended to her own life. If you are a primary caregiver, I encourage you to follow her example: look after yourself as well as the one you're caring for.

HELP BY LENDING HOPE

In *Apprenticed to Hope,* Julie Neraas writes about a friend of hers who was making slow progress in recovery from childhood sexual abuse:

> Healing was threading its way, inch by incremental inch, through her psyche and body, though she could not yet see or feel it. The therapist proposed that my friend borrow hope from her for a while, until the day came when she could take it in to herself enough to be warmed by its flame. In essence, she threw her client a buoy and my friend grabbed on.[50]

Neraas showed me how the hope that others have in my recovery helps me stay hopeful, especially at times when things aren't going well. To really help, this hope needs to be realistic, credible, and tough—not hope for recovery overnight or for recovery without struggle, but hope for recovery as it can actually happen. If you have doubts about your own ability to offer realistic hope (and I think such hope is an essential for a primary caregiver), NAMI classes and programs are good places to look for help. NAMI is all about realistic and credible hope for recovery. When people show such hope by their words, actions, and attitude, their hope is indeed a buoy one can grab on to.

HELP BY GIVING A FOOT MASSAGE

In *Let Your Life Speak*, Parker Palmer tells about a friend named Bill who visited him in a time of deep depression. Every afternoon Bill came to his home and gave him a foot massage. Palmer writes, "He found the one place in my body where I could still experience feeling—and feel somewhat reconnected with the human race."[51]

Bill didn't say much during these visits, but what he did say gently responded to Palmer's condition.

> [Bill] would say, "I can sense your struggle today," or, "It feels like you are getting stronger." I could not always respond, but his words were deeply helpful: they reassured me that I could still be seen by *someone* —life-giving knowledge in the midst of an experience that makes one feel annihilated and invisible.[52]

With his regular visits and supportive words—always honest, encouraging when possible—Bill stands as an example of how to care for someone living with mental illness. His faithfulness reassured Palmer that he has not fallen off the edge of the human race. Showing up, bringing credible hope, Bill is a teacher for anyone who seeks to help.

Bill also teaches us that helping someone living with mental illness need not be complicated. In the early months of my recovery, I found so much pleasure in simply watching a basketball or baseball game with one of my children or a good friend. I'm not sure watching a game on TV would appear on anyone's list of how to help someone living with depression, but for me these were wonderful times: time with people that had few social demands, an event on the schedule that I could look forward to, and an easy way to connect with normal life.

As my recovery progressed and I was comfortable being with a wider range of people, I was fortunate to have a number of friends who reached out to me. Friends asked me whether I wanted to go for a walk around the lake, have coffee at my favorite coffee shop (and they'd pay), go for a ride in their new car, check out a movie, attend some event at their church, or have lunch together (sometimes with the offer to pay and sometimes without). These weren't friends like Bill, who took on major caregiving roles, but more casual friends who wanted to show they cared about me and had not abandoned me. If you're in this more casual role with someone living with mental illness, I hope these examples will help you to find your own way to help.

Help 42

Facing Shame

After Susan and I were married, we had a studio apartment close to the University of Minnesota, where she was completing her Bachelor of Science in Nursing degree, and I was going to graduate school in philosophy. With a limited budget, we shopped for groceries at a railroad-salvage store and scanned the paper for coupons and other ways to save. So it happened that we came across a deal for free steak knives. We weren't eating much steak, but who could pass up free steak knives? Besides, they had to be sharp enough to slice Spam. To get the knives, we committed to listening to a salesman make a sales pitch for various types of pots, pans, and utensils— a small price to pay for free steak knives.

Sue made an appointment for the salesman to come by our apartment early one evening. I had a test the next day, so we agreed that I'd hide in the bathroom and study while she endured the pointless sales pitch. There was no other place to hide in the apartment, except maybe under the bed. We had a plan, but the salesman had persistence. He showed up on time, but after a while it became clear that he didn't know when to leave. He was determined to make a sale to people who had neither interest nor money. What we thought would be a fifteen-minute sales pitch passed the hour mark with no sign of slowing down.

In the meantime, I was getting bored and cramped in the bathroom. The toilet seat is OK to sit on to study for a while, but it's not a recliner. And what if the salesman asked to use the bathroom? Oops! We hadn't thought this one through. No way could we ask him to go outside; it was January in Minnesota. Moreover, as the salesman became more desperate, he upped the volume until I felt like he was in the bathroom with me. Hard to study

Immanuel Kant when some guy is screaming in your ear about his revolutionary pots and the miracle of Teflon.

Finally, after he had to have set some kind of record for the length of a failed sales pitch, the salesman admitted defeat in the face of Sue's resolute sales resistance. After one last effort—I think he was willing to throw in some lobster forks—he finally left. As soon as the door closed, I rushed out of the bathroom to admire our four brand-new steak knives, complete with ill-fitting plastic handles and a spiffy cardboard box to keep them in.

That's it. This story is self-illustrating, just the kind of story someone would write who had read Kant a long time ago. Hiding in the bathroom and letting Sue do the heavy lifting—I don't come off a hero, more like a lowlife. I'm OK with that. This is one of those stories where I make fun of myself, not with malice, but just because it's so damn funny. And when I tell it, I always laugh louder than anybody else. No way could I have been free to tell it when depression had control over my life. Being able to tell this story about myself is a progress marker in my recovery.

I have come a long way. For so much of my life, I couldn't stop scrutinizing myself, holding up every flaw under a merciless microscope, awash with shame that someone would find a minute imperfection. I was always careful not to reveal anything about myself until I had totally vetted what I was going to say. I would do my best to guess how other people would think about me after I opened up a little about myself or told a story about something I'd done. Was there anything in the story that might reflect badly on the image I was trying to maintain? Was there anything, ever so tiny, that might make me cringe when I thought about it later? Was it a safe story to tell? With such strict criteria, I didn't tell many stories.

In *I Thought It Was Just Me (but it isn't)*, Dr. Brené Brown says this kind of behavior is based on the avoidance of shame. Summing up a number of interviews with people who struggled with the same anxiety over the imagined opinions of others as I do, she writes:

> As these phrases indicate, shame is about perception. Shame is how we see ourselves through other people's eyes. When I Interviewed women about shame experiences, it was always about "how others see me" or "what others think."[53]

As I write this book, I fantasize about a going on a book tour and becoming a beloved celebrity. Oprah would go back on TV just to interview me. But I also imagine doing a reading where an embarrassingly small crowd loathes the book. "This is all obvious and derivative." "The more I read your book, the worse I felt." "A depressing book about depression." And finally the dreaded, "You should be ashamed of yourself for writing this." And I am. I can literally feel my throat tighten and the blood rushing to my face as I write this. I've made a lot progress, but shame is powerful and tenacious.

Brown writes, "When it comes to shame, understanding is a prerequisite for change."[54] I think back over how I was raised and how early on I was taught to look at myself through other people's eyes. Of course, my family wasn't unique in teaching this, but I do think there was something about my family, especially about how my dad felt as a country boy trying to get ahead in the city, that intensified the lesson. He was a fiercely proud man, and I believe this was a cover for being ashamed of his country accent, his sketchy grammar, and his lack of a college education. He achieved a lot in his life, much that he could indeed have been proud of, but I believe shame kept him from fully enjoying his successes.

Sometimes I understand shame as the place where my depression and anxiety come together. Shame feeds my anxiety by emphasizing that something I do or say will embarrass me, and it feeds my depression by diminishing my self-worth and ability to enjoy life. I've used many of these Forty-Nine Helps to free myself from the imagined opinions of other people. As I've become more secure in the love of family and friends, I've worried less about what other people think. I have learned from my therapists how I overreact to anything that might verge on criticism. I know from cognitive behavioral therapy that it's pointless to try to mind read other people, thinking I can tell what they're thinking about me. I know from all the work I've done to counter perfectionism that we all make mistakes and that embarrassment is part of the human condition. I know all these things, but shame has deep roots.

I'm not sure what happened to those four free steak knives. I hope they found a good home, though I wish sometimes that we'd kept one of them. I'd like to look at it from time to time—to remember the salesman who wouldn't go away and to ask myself why it took me so long to tell the story of how Sue defeated him while I skulked in the bathroom.

Help 43

Claiming Rights and Accepting Responsibilities

In writing about rights and responsibilities, I mean these terms as they apply to participating in one's own treatment and recovery. In the hospital, I simply did what I was told and took the pills I was given. If someone had shown me a patient's bill of rights, I would not have understood it. Today, far from being so passive, I am an active participant in my own recovery, embracing the rights and responsibilities that come with it. This can be a challenge, but, like anything that enhances one's freedom of choice, it nurtures self-worth and self-respect.

In her book *Living with Depression*, Deborah Serani writes, "*Psychotherapy cannot be successful unless you want to be there.*"[55] I agree, and I take this as part of my rights and responsibilities. As a person with self-respect and agency, I have the right to choose what I want to do, and this includes whether to do therapy. I am quick to add that if I had not chosen to participate in therapy, my recovery would have suffered greatly. Still, having the choice is important. My recovery would also have suffered if my right to choose had not been respected.

With the exercise of this right, I also took on responsibilities for my recovery. Serani writes, "*Psychotherapy will not fix you. You will fix you. A psychotherapist's task is to help you help yourself.*"[56] My therapy wouldn't have gone anywhere unless I had taken the responsibility to be an active participant. It took me a little while to take this ownership, but when I did, when I started to open up and tell my therapist what was really hurting me, my therapy began to make my life better.

The dialogue between rights and responsibilities is part of the ongoing therapeutic process. From the beginning, we have the right to ask questions and to participate in creating a treatment plan. It's our life, and we have the right to ensure that the goals of the treatment are what we want for our lives. We also have the right to know why a particular medication is being prescribed for us and what the side effects might be. If we feel, for whatever reason, that our therapist is not helping us, we have the right to seek someone else and to be assured of continuity of care.

Reciprocally, we have the responsibility to be on time for our appointments and to give the agreed upon notification if we are forced to cancel. Once we have accepted a treatment plan, we have the responsibility to participate as fully as we are able and to be as forthright as we can if we feel the plan needs to be changed. If our therapist assigns us homework, then we have the right to question how it fits into our treatment plan and goals. If our questions are satisfactorily answered, then we have the responsibility to do as much of it as we can. We also have the responsibility to take the medications we have agreed to take in the dosages and at the times prescribed. If something isn't going well in our recovery, including having a reaction to a medication, we have the responsibility, as well as the right, to notify our therapist or psychiatrist.

As we are able, we also have a responsibility to learn about our illness. This allows us to be more effective participants in our own recovery. I've emphasized how much I've learned from other people living with mental illness, beginning in the hospital and continuing with my community at Vail Place. I've also learned a lot from NAMI workshops and groups. Reading is a pleasure for me, a recovery aid in itself, and much of what I've learned about my illness has come from books. From the quotations I have included and the bibliography, you can tell which authors and books I have found particularly helpful. In addition, the NAMI website www.nami.org will lead you to a wealth of helpful written materials as well as to some amazing podcasts.

Looking at recovery in terms of rights and responsibilities can help us to throw light on dark places. I think back to the moment just before my first hospitalization when my struggle with suicidal thoughts led me to call my wife and ask for help. Though I don't understand why I chose to call her rather than follow through with my thoughts, the language of rights and responsibilities illuminates what happened.

In this language, I had a right to call Sue because she is my wife. This feels strange to say, not the usual way of talking about a marriage, but our commitment to each other, spoken in marriage vows and lived out for decades, made her the person I felt I had the right to call, the person I could ask to share the burden of the pain that was threatening to take my life. If I had not reached her, would I have called one of our adult children, with whom I have different but also deep and abiding ties? I don't know. I hope so, but I don't know.

I also believe that I had a responsibility to call her. Even while I hated myself, I still knew that taking my life would cause so much pain to her and our children. Did I not have the responsibility to reach out, to tell her, and at least to give her a chance to help? I believe so, and I'm forever grateful that I did. If you are ever in such a place, please reach out to one of those people you have the strongest ties with. You owe it to them.

I know that I personalize, taking responsibility for far more than is appropriate or even logical. In writing this Help I've tried to be wary of doing this. But if I find personal responsibility where none actually exists, that doesn't mean I don't have real responsibilities or that I don't benefit by claiming them. I continue to sort out what my responsibilities are, just as I continue to sort out what my rights are. This has helped bring clarity and direction to my recovery.

Help 44

Doing the Right Thing

IN HIS BOOK *INTO Thin Air*, Jon Krakauer describes the disaster created by a blizzard on Mount Everest in May 1996. Before it was over, eight climbers had died on the mountain, including members of a party organized by the Indo-Tibetan border police. As two of the party members lay close to death, members of another group who were pushing hard to make the summit came upon them. They did not share food, water, or bottled oxygen; they just left the climbers there to die. Later, when one of those men who had walked by was interviewed, he tried to explain, "We were too tired to help. Above 8,000 meters is not a place where people can afford morality."[57]

When I read this, my first reactions were horror and then contempt for climbers who chose to pass by on the other side. They seemed so hell-belt on reaching the summit they lost any sense of compassion toward others. But in recovery, I've learned to be slow to judge. Though they had bottled oxygen, maybe their supply was inadequate; maybe they were oxygen deprived, unable to reason clearly enough to practice morality. After all, I have had my own experience of being in a place where morality did not apply to me. As I sat in the hospital ER lost in pain, about to be involuntarily committed to a psych unit, deciding about morality or duty (whatever duty might have looked like in such a place) would have been impossible. Duty? I couldn't think straight. I was about to be judged a danger to myself and others. I had dropped out of the moral universe.

During this mental health crisis, it would have been absurd to talk with me about morality, just as it would have been absurd to talk with me about rights and responsibilities. I am now in a different place, back in the moral universe where questions of morality and duty do apply to me.

Indeed, I believe that focusing on these questions can be a help in recovery. I also believe that it is important to be careful in doing so. In the hospital we talked about what it feels like when morality degenerates into a long list of "should statements," so you end up shoulding all over yourself. David Burns writes about the emotional consequences of shoulds:

> Should statements generate a lot of unnecessary emotional turmoil in your daily life. When the reality of your own behavior falls short of your standards, your shoulds and shouldn'ts create self-loathing, shame, and guilt. When the all-too-human performance of other people falls short of your expectations, as will inevitably happen from time to time, you'll feel bitter and self-righteous. You'll either have to change your expectations to approximate reality or always feel let down by human behavior.[58]

Burns does an excellent job of pointing out all the dangers of shoulding. We have seen how the factors he cites—expectations and human fallibility, as well as the dread trinity of "self-loathing, shame, and guilt"—can scuttle one's recovery. As we move into the moral universe and claim certain values as our own, we need to be cautious. When our attempts to do the right thing fall short, we need to show ourselves compassion, avoiding the dread trinity that does so much harm. We need to treat other people's moral failures with similar compassion. As citizens of the moral universe, we need to be understanding, not demanding perfection, but accepting human limitations.

With this caution in place, I can now say that I have benefited greatly by claiming my dignity and self-respect as a moral agent in the world. Something about how we are as human beings, how we are hard wired, makes it deeply satisfying to live in accordance with the values we have chosen.

One value I live by: I tell the truth. When exhaustion, anxiety, and the inability to think clearly kept me from meeting my work and life responsibilities, I regularly lied to cover for myself. Of course I beat up on myself afterward—always mentally, sometimes physically—for being contemptible.

As lying was part of my illness, so telling the truth has been part of my recovery. It is a cornerstone of my healthy identity, a huge enhancer of my self-esteem and self-respect. Who am I? I am a person who tells the truth. I admire this about myself, and it is another marker of how far my recovery has progressed. I try to accept my imperfections and admit that a convenient lie still slips in now and again. I do my best to own the lie, make amends if it's serious, and then forgive myself and move on. This happens, but telling the truth is now my custom, my default position, and it is that way even when there's a significant cost to my being honest. I feel really good about being a truth teller. I'm going to hold on to that feeling.

Another value I live by: I try to help other people. I have no idea what I would do on a mountain at eight thousand meters. I know there was a time in my illness when I could help neither other people nor myself, but I'm not in the hospital now. I'm standing on level ground. I am able to make my own decisions, and I simply feel better when I help other people. These days my main way of helping other people is to tell my story of illness and recovery. Doing this is also part of who I am, and it is who I want to be.

Living according to these values gives me pleasure. It's as simple as that. I like and respect myself as someone who's at least trying to do the right thing. That's a simple claim, yet fundamental to my happiness. I speak from my own experience about what has furthered my recovery. I also know that many people we look to for moral guidance—including Rabbi Kushner, Bishop Tutu, and the Dalai Lama—have in their different ways brought forward the deep connection between feeling good about ourselves and doing good toward others.

In writing this book, I have vacillated between including this Help and deleting it. My ambivalence is about the danger of shoulds, the human tendency to make incessant moral demands. With caution against this danger, I've chosen to include it. For me, moral agency and self-worth are tightly bound together. By practicing morality, I have grown stronger in self-worth. I want to offer what I have learned to help others,

Help 45

Finding Common Ground

YEARS AGO SUE AND I traveled with our younger son to visit our older son, who was studying painting in Santa Fe, New Mexico. I love being a tour guide, and I had planned our trip so we wouldn't miss a thing. Once we started, I pushed hard so we made the absolute best use of our time, which meant that we didn't waste good sightseeing hours on distracting trivialities like stopping for lunch. This inevitably led to some awkward hungry moments between my family and me.

So it was that in New Mexico we found ourselves zipping along the highway well past noon, not only without lunch, but with no visible options for lunch in the future. Just when simmering family discontent threatened to burst into open rebellion, we came to a small town in the center of which was a Baptist Church with a sign out front: "Community Lunch Today. 11:00 a.m.–1:30 p.m. All Are Welcome." Great! Lunch and helping a church's fundraiser. It was already a little past 1:30 p.m., so we had to act fast. I hit the brakes and swerved into the little parking lot. We charged into the church.

You could see they were beginning to shut down, but there was still food, and a server beckoned us over. Lunch was served cafeteria style—a meal of baked chicken, green beans, and mashed potatoes with gravy. We were also given a sizable slab of brownie and the choice of milk or coffee. The dining room was almost empty, but then again it was getting late. The food was simple, warm, and hearty.

After a few bites to assuage the worst of my hunger, I looked around to check the place out. There were a few older folks, mostly sitting alone and sipping a last cup of coffee. But there was also a Hispanic family, a mom and four small children, finishing their desserts. One of the older folks was wearing a much-stained sport coat and another seemed agitated, but the overall feeling of the place was comfortable and welcoming, a classic church-basement dining room, even a picture of Jesus and the little children hanging a little crookedly on the wall.

After we were done, and the family rebellion against my tour leadership put off for at least one more day, I went to thank the servers. Also, since nobody had asked us for money, I assumed this was the kind of church dinner where you made a donation instead of paying a set fee for a ticket. I went back into the kitchen and found the server who had first beckoned to us. When I asked her where to pay, she laughed and said, "You don't have to pay anything. It's just as our sign says, 'All Are Welcome.' There is a lot of poverty in this town and in this part of New Mexico. It's part of our church mission to offer a free lunch to anyone who comes in. I'm just thankful you and your family got here in time to get something hot to eat."

Maybe, if we hadn't been in a rush, I would have figured out that the free meal was a community service for those who had difficulty making ends meet. Families who were hungry only because of my tour guiding were not the intended recipients. And maybe it was clear when we came in that we didn't really need a free meal—if the church members had seen us drive up in our upgraded rental car, it would have been clear—but they made no exceptions. They welcomed us, fed us, and treated us as guests.

The server was working while we talked. I felt awkward trying to explain that we'd made a mistake, and I didn't want to reject their hospitality. Besides, had we really made a mistake? We were indeed hungry, and they were offering food. I did tell her we were grateful for the good meal and asked if I could make a donation to support their program. She smiled and said it wasn't necessary, but they never turned down donations. I made my donation, and as soon as we were all back in the car, I explained to my family the nature of the meal we enjoyed. Of course, the boys teased me for doing all I could to save money, but like Sue and me, they were impressed and grateful to the church people who fed us.

This is a story about similarity and difference. My family and I, middle-class people on vacation, were different economically from the people who the church lunch program was designed to help. I know nothing of the stories of the few people who were still in the dining room when we got there, but I'm pretty sure that they did not have the financial advantages that we did. It was a fluke that we'd ended up in the dining hall; I'm guessing it was a necessity for the other guests.

Similar economic difference exists between me and many other people living with mental illness. Of course, there are people living with mental illness in all economic brackets, but mental illness is exacerbated by economic insecurity. Having adequate financial resources shields a person from many of the stressors that make recovery more difficult.

It's true that I endured hell in the hospital waiting room. But it's also true that I wasn't in that waiting room very long before a doctor came. We had good insurance, enough to cover the costs of a private hospital. Since then, I have met so many people living with mental illness who do not have good insurance or who do not have insurance at all. I remember talking to a young woman who had waited for hours in the waiting room of a public hospital before she could see someone. "I was suicidal," she said. "There was no one watching me. I could have so easily have run out into the street and stepped in front of the next car."

In my therapy group the first time I was in the hospital, I heard the story of a woman who had endured regular sexual harassment on her job. I respected her for telling the truth about this and other hard circumstances of her life. Her truth telling encouraged my truth telling. She had made good progress in recovery and was about to be discharged. This should have been good news, but it wasn't. It meant going back to the job where she had been harassed. She felt she had no other option, even though she knew going back there might undo all the progress she had made and land her back in the hospital.

Adequate income shields a person from so many stressors. I have a safe place to live. I took that for granted until I met people living with mental illness who didn't have the most basic apartment even though they qualify for assistance, because such an apartment is simply not to be found. Though I worried mightily about money, with Sue's income as an RN and my denomination's disability program, my worry was more a symptom of my illness than a statement of our reality. For so many living with mental illness, hampered by a checkered work history, lack of money is a real-world barrier to recovery and well-being. Barring changes that will make our society more economically just and compassionate, economic insecurity will continue to make life more stressful for people who need our help.

There are more ways that I am different from a lot of people living with mental illness: I'm white, heterosexual, male, and able-bodied. I'm spared from many kinds of discrimination faced by people who are different from me, discrimination that is often heaped on top of the stigma of being mental ill. Likewise, I am not an addict; I do not have a criminal record; I do not exhibit obvious symptoms. By no means do I claim any of these characteristics as some kind of accomplishment on my part. I have advantage and privilege that I've done nothing to deserve.

These differences are real, but my similarities with other people who suffer from mental illness go deeper. This brings me back to that church dining hall in New Mexico. My family and I were different from the intended recipients. That's undeniable. But like the others who shared the dining hall with us, we were hungry and needed to be fed. We shared a common human bond, deeper than what made us different.

I feel the same way about other people living with mental illness. I know I was born with advantages, but I also live with mental illness. This bond is stronger than our differences. I feel this when I go into Vail Place and talk heart to heart with a member. Differences slip away. What we face together unites us.

Help 46

Managing Depression

I CHOOSE NOT TO do some things because I live with a mental illness. I've heard about jobs, even been invited to apply for some, that I have chosen not to seek out because I felt the stress and demands of those positions would exacerbate my depression. I've chosen not to go to some large social gatherings with many former parishioners out of concern that the demands to fill a lot of people in on what I've been doing recently, implicitly on how I've been doing mentally, would be exhausting and not good for me. I've let a few friendships lapse because they were too tied up with the causes of my depression. I think these were all good decisions.

I realize this Help is in some tension with many of the others. Starting with my time in the ER, I have been telling my story of moving back into the world and working to create a life that is more joyous and satisfying than the one I led before being hospitalized. In recovery, I've learned to say yes to all that's good in life, reclaiming the joy that depression tried to steal from me.

This Help is about saying no. It's about not doing things that might be good in themselves—like taking a new job or going to a social event—but are not good for me in my recovery. Though this might sound like a step backwards, I believe the opposite: saying no can be an act of self-worth by asserting that one's happiness is too valuable to be put at risk.

I'm much influenced in this by what happened after my hospitalizations. I twice tried to return to the church I had served for so long. The first time, I managed only a couple of days before my rapidly returning symptoms became too much for me to manage. The church then gave me three months off, after which I tried once more to return. That time, the very commitment to return, even before I had gone back into the building, reenergized all my symptoms. After a few terrible days, I was back on the same psych unit.

All of this was scary. It was also scary to learn that each time one has such a severe depressive episode, the odds increase that another episode will occur. This learning was reinforced for me when I read about cortisol, the primary stress hormone. In *The Noonday Demon*, Andrew Solomon writes:

> Once you've had a stress sufficient to cause a protracted increase of your cortisol levels, your cortisol system is damaged, and in the future it will not readily turn off once it has been activated. Thereafter, the elevation of cortisol after a small trauma may not normalize as it would under ordinary circumstances. Like anything that has been broken once, the cortisol system is prone to break again and again, with less and less external pressure.[59]

My second severe depressive episode and what I had learned about its increasing the odds of still more episodes meant I could not dismiss my first hospitalization as some kind of perfect mental storm, so rare I'd never have to worry about such an event occurring again. What had happened once had indeed happened again. It had marked me both mentally and physically, and it was far too dangerous to be minimized in any way. After my second hospitalization, it would be more than a year before I returned to work, and then I went to a different place for a limited time period.

Given my history, it's fair to say that fear of another hospitalization led me into the kind of depression management where I say no to situations that feel risky for my recovery. Many people living with depression practice some form of risk control. Deborah Serani, a psychologist who also lives with depression, writes about her own therapy:

> I came to learn how to avoid stressors that would worsen my moods (taking on too much in a day, not delegating enough responsibility to others, limiting my social calendar, for example) or experiences that would set me up for another depressive episode (watching too much television news, not exercising enough, allowing fearful thoughts to win without a fight.)[60]

The first time I read Serani's description I laughed. I had felt guilty about avoiding too much TV news, as if I'm avoiding my responsibility to be a well-informed citizen. I'm quick to add that I'm a devoted newspaper reader—this admission may date me more than anything else in this book—but TV news, with every crisis in living color and somebody screaming about tomorrow's apocalypse, is just too stressful. Serani helped me see that I've been practicing depression management unawares and that I have no reason to feel guilty.

Though I am now aware of what I've been doing, I still found it reassuring to read that Serani seeks to control stress by not taking on too much in a day. I try to do the same: on a day when stress is piling up, I start putting things off until tomorrow. Like a lot of depression management, this is an art more than an exact science. It involves balancing the real-world determination of what can be put off until tomorrow—taxes are due April 15—with my inner determination of whether I'm wisely managing my depression or simply avoiding what I don't want to do. I'm getting better at this, though sometimes I still get it wrong. Then I pay the price of undue stress or a missed deadline. It's also true that sometimes I get a break: taxes are due on April 15 unless you get an extension. Even the real world can be a little forgiving sometimes.

The same need to balance things out is true in saying yes or no to possible jobs, a part of the art of my depression management where getting it wrong can have serious consequences. There have been moments on jobs I've taken since my hospitalizations when I've wondered whether I hadn't miscalculated the risk. The stress of the job seemed greater than the gain. I've spent some pretty rough nights because of this, once again running scenarios in my head that featured me as the failure, the one to blame.

Fortunately, these bad times did not develop into a mental health crisis. I now have sufficient resilience not to let heavy stress at work push me back into a crisis. I have learned to accept my limits and to let go of perfectionism. Most of all, I have learned to tell trusted people when I am hurting and to get their help in difficult times.

Finally, saying no is the assertion of a right, a manifestation of self-respect, and a way to establish personal boundaries. In *An Altar in the World*, Barbara Brown Taylor offers saying no as a spiritual practice. She quotes the theologian Karl Barth, "A being is only free when it can determine and limit its activity."[61] I claim this freedom; I have the right to say no. Of course I do, but for me, in the context of all that has happened in my life, saying no feels revolutionary and deeply healthy. Walt Whitman would be proud of me: "I celebrate myself."[62]

Help 47

Fighting Stigma

I HATE THE SPITTOON. The spittoon I'm referring to is a prop in *Rio Bravo*,[63] the classic John Ford western that we watched one night on the psych unit. Dean Martin and Ricky Nelson are in the movie, which means there are memorable cowboy duets. Of course some of us sang along—well, kind of—to "Get Along Home, Cindy, Cindy" and "My Rifle, My Saddle, and Me." I wonder what somebody would have felt who walked in right in the middle of our singing about my rifle, saddle, etc. My best guess is they would have zipped their Minnesota Vikings jacket right back up, reversed course, and gone back out the door before we'd gotten through the chorus. Some people just don't like good music.

For me the most memorable scene in the movie involves Dude, Dean Martin's character. He's an alcoholic who's trying his best to get sober with precious little support from anyone. It's just too much, and his resolve finally crumbles. The saloon door is always open, and Dude goes back inside. He's trembling for a drink, but he's flat broke. Taunting him so all the bar-flies can yuck it up, one of the bad guys flips a coin into a full spittoon. Will Dude humiliate himself and stick his hand into the spit to get the money for a drink?

At that moment, a patient in a Minnesota Twins hat got up and started screaming at Dude not to do it. "Don't let them take away your dignity. Screw all the bastards." In the end Dude doesn't do it. I wish that had been because he came to himself and asserted his self-respect, but that's not what happens. The sheriff (of course he is played by John Wayne) strides into the saloon and kicks the spittoon over. Call it tough love? Later Dude gets his revenge by tossing a coin into the spittoon and making the guy who'd ridiculed him fish it out. We cheered our heads off.

Dude's alcoholism puts his sense of personal dignity and self-respect in jeopardy. Depression did that for me. I think about the experience of being hospitalized, of being stripped of my belt, razor, shoelaces, notebook, and freedom. I think about abandoning a job and all the commitments I had made to people. I think about so many things I did and said, and I shudder. My depression did its best to destroy my self-respect.

Recovery has been about getting my self-respect back again. That's why I hate stigma. When I hear the word mentioned in conjunction with mental illness, I immediately think of the spittoon. It makes me want to channel John Wayne and kick the spittoon (aka stigma) as far as possible. Then I want to go where the spittoon lands and kick it again. After another kick or two, I want to pick it up and look at all the dents I've made. I'm feeling better already.

Stigma allies itself with the mental illness. It does its best to strip away dignity and self-respect. As you work to stop blaming and shaming yourself, stigma says, "Hold on a minute. Know what? You really are to blame for your mental illness. You're just so much weaker than other people, such a coward. If you just got off your ass and made more of an effort, you could get over it. Many people are worse off than you are. So suck it up and get back to work." If you listen to this toxic message, a message of pure evil, your recovery will wither. Stigma really is the spittoon. In recovery we learn to kick it over.

NAMI has been in the forefront of exposing the lies stigma tells and in giving us tools to fight these lies. At the NAMI website www.nami.org, you will find a great deal of help in combating stigma. Like everything else in recovery, we need help in fighting stigma. NAMI is that help.

NAMI encourages us to speak openly about our mental illness. By doing this, you teach people through your personal example that there is nothing to be ashamed of. In fighting stigma, people living with mental illness have tremendous power. As you can, as your recovery allows, I encourage you to be open about your mental illness.

NAMI also encourages us to be open about whatever treatment we're receiving. On the NAMI blog "Fight Mental Health Stigma," Yasabel Gracia is quoted as saying, "Why can people say they have an appointment with their primary care doctor without fear of being judged, but this lack of fear does not apply when it comes to mental health professionals?"[64] Exactly.

A similar anti-stigma strategy that NAMI suggests is to encourage parity between physical and mental illness. I know my own self-stigmatizing took a major blow when my therapist told me my mental illness was a disease like diabetes or heart disease. This is obvious to me now, but at that time it was a revelation. I use the comparison when I tell others about my depression. The more we help other people understand mental illness as an illness, the more effective we'll be in pushing back against stigma.

Several of the Forty-Nine Helps—practicing compassion, using non-judgmental language in talking about mental illness, owning one's own story, cultivating self-worth, being authentic—are also ways to fight stigma. This makes sense: stigma allies with mental illness, so when we fight one, we also fight the other. Our self-esteem and self-respect grow when we confront stigma head on and show we are not afraid of it. Fear gives stigma power; courage strips that power away.

Nevertheless, I confess that sometimes I am tempted to slack off in the fight against stigma. You get tired of fighting the same battle over and over. Besides, many of the people I'm closest to are part of some kind of mental health community. With them, stigma is such an obvious evil there is no need to call attention to it, so I can lull myself into the false belief that the battle against stigma has been won.

When I'm tempted to do this, I remember the button I was given to wear when a group of Vail Place friends and I went to our state capitol in St. Paul. With NAMI members from all over the state, we gathered to work for mental health parity. We lobbied legislators for a variety of bills that would improve the lives of people living with mental illness. The button has a life preserver on it and "787." That's the number of Minnesotans who died by suicide in 2018—a reality that jolts me out of my incipient apathy and sends me back to fighting stigma.

Help 48

Surviving the Worst That Could Happen

My friend on the psych unit, the woman who shared her mixed nuts with me and cautioned me not to take my eyes off pleasure, told me, "Bob, my meltdown was the worst thing and the best thing that ever happened to me." Looking back, I can say the same. As we come near the end of this book, after describing how much my meltdown hurt and how much it has cost me, I believe it is clear why I agree with her about its being the worst thing.

But what about the best thing? How can it be both the worst and the best? My marriage, the gift of our children, the abiding love of close friends—there have been other "best things" in my life, so I'm tempted to back off and qualify my agreement with her. But I'd still say that my meltdown, though a personal disaster, has been one of the best things in my life.

My reason for saying this has much in common with how author and commentator Karen Armstrong describes the worst and best thing in her own life. In her autobiography, *The Spiral Staircase*, she writes about her temporal lobe epilepsy diagnosis, "The worst had happened, but that meant that I no longer had anything much to lose, and increasingly I found that quite liberating."[65] It's the freedom we all feel when we can say, "After all, what have I got to lose?"

My meltdown freed me in the same way that a blast of dynamite demolishes the old and frees a building site for new construction. My former life had been blown all to hell. My position, reputation, and security—all that I had sacrificed decades to secure—were left like construction debris ready to be carted off to the landfill. I had nothing left to lose.

Then I woke up the next morning, and I wasn't dead. As they say, it was the first day of the rest of my life. It took me some time to realize that I was free—it's hard to feel free when you're heavily medicated and locked behind a door—but the realization came. My old life had been demolished, but I wasn't trapped somewhere under the rubble. I was still alive, and I was free to start over. To use Armstrong's words, it was all "quite liberating." I didn't know it at the time, but the delicious bacon, crispy but not dry, that I had with my first breakfast on the psych unit was actually the main course of a celebratory meal.

Freedom for me in recovery has meant the freedom to change. The basic trajectory of this change has been moving from living inside my head, constantly spinning illogical scenarios and struggling with phantoms, to living in the real world. To put it another way, I've changed from living in ever-increasing fear that I could never talk about, to talking about my fear and becoming less afraid. Also I've changed from incessantly worrying about what other people might think about me to simply being who I am and not worrying about what others think. None of these changes are complete. Whatever life I'm building is still under construction. But by this point, with a lot of help, my life is actually starting to look pretty good, though it still needs quite a bit of landscaping.

This revelation, freedom amidst the rubble, has been the best thing about my meltdown. As I have learned to enjoy this freedom, I have been guided by what my meltdown taught me. Like everyone who has had a mental health crisis, everyone who knows what it is like to lose utter control of life, I learned that I have a breaking point. In recovery I am diligent to ensure that the breaking does not happen again. I say no when I feel a choice will trigger serious stress, when I think a situation will draw me close to my breaking point. I don't know where that point is, but I know exactly what it feels like when I get close.

Just as knowing that I have a breaking point has taught me depression management, it has also taught me not to take feeling good and enjoying life for granted. I know how bad life can be. Knowing that, I savor every joy when life is good. I know what it's like to feel powerless and helpless, so now I am amazed at how resilient and adaptable I actually can be. I know what it's like to burn hot with shame, so now I am deeply pleased to be able to tell the story of my illness and defy that shame. I know what it's like to feel like a fraud, so now I feel deep satisfaction in telling the truth about my illness. I know what it's like to feel useless, so now I find deep joy in helping people.

Writing this book is another means by which I've sought to help people. In doing so, I've experienced feelings similar to those described by Scot Stossel in *My Age of Anxiety*.

> Yet writing this book has required me to wallow in my shame, anxiety, and weakness so that I can properly capture and convey them—an experience that has only reinforced how deep and long-standing my anxiety and vulnerability are.[66]

At times in my writing, as I tried to be as honest about what happened and what pain that has caused me, I've felt I was doing my own kind of wallowing in depression and anxiety. I've needed to be clear about depression's devastation, so I can be clear about recovery's joy. To manage the stress of this work, I've taken my time and backed away when necessary. The cost— the personal price of putting on paper the worst thing that ever happened to me—feels well worth the effort. Having paid the cost, I can write credibly about the joy of recovery. In so doing, I hope I have helped you and other readers.

I come back to that simple phrase in Psalm 30: "Weeping may endure for the night, but joy cometh in the morning" (Psalm 30:5b). I've learned there is no way I can deny or hide from the weeping. I tried, and it overwhelmed me. But there is also joy. This is the best thing in my recovery story. If you look after it, if you refuse to take it for granted, and if you treat it with respect, joy will stay for a long, long time.

HELP 49

Being Well

SEVERE DEPRESSION IS CRUEL, invasive, and total. Far worse than the dragons faced by St. Martha and St. George, it's a dragon that breathes fire into your mind. The fire melts thoughts until they flow together—white heat and terrible pain. It consumes all the good things: sleep and appetite, the ability to concentrate and pay attention, the capacity to know pleasure and share love. All that's left is pure pain. You learn as a little child to snatch your hand away from the fire. How do you do that when the fire is in your mind?

Whatever I suggest, imply, or point out about how badly I hurt when my depression raged—it was worse than that. This is my truth about depression. For one final time in these Forty-Nine Helps, I want to be emphatic about that.

It's also true that fourteen years have passed since my last hospitalization. Some days the pain has come back, though not as severe or terrifying, but such bad days have become far less frequent, and I know who to ask for help when the pain returns. Most days I like my life, and I like myself. Given what depression has done to me, it's incredible that I can claim I enjoy being alive.

In a way this joy has been about getting back what depression took away from me. Let's take stock: Appetite restored? Check—though one med overdid it, causing me to pack on the pounds. Sleep returned? Check—at least most nights. Ability to concentrate and pay attention back up and running? Check—though my spouse might disagree when we're going over today's to-do list. Mood lightened and pleasure returned? Check—most days. Self-harm ended? Check—almost completely. No longer wanting to die? Check—and check again.

The National Institute of Mental Health (NIMH) lists these signs and symptoms of depression on its website, ww.nimh.nih.gov/health/publications/depression/index.shtml:

Persistent sad, anxious, or empty mood

Feelings of hopelessness and pessimism

Feelings of guilt, worthlessness, or helplessness

Loss of interest or pleasure in hobbies and activities

Decreased energy, fatigue, or being "slowed down"

Difficulty concentrating, remembering, or making decisions

Feeling restless or having trouble sitting still

Difficulty concentrating, remembering, or making decisions

Difficulty sleeping, early-morning awakening, or oversleeping

Appetite and/or weight changes

Thoughts of death or suicide or suicide attempts

Restlessness or irritablity

Aches or pains, headaches, cramps or digestive problems without a clear physical cause and/or that do not ease even with treatment[67]

Checking my recovery against this list of symptoms, seeing how much my symptoms have diminished or even disappeared from my life, I am even more assured that my recovery has come a long way. I invite you to do the same, using this list to better understand the status of your own recovery. I hope that after you do this, you too will come away with increased confidence that your recovery is going well.

Given the progress I have made in my recovery, can I say that I have recovered from my major depression and anxiety disorder? I can't, or won't, say yes. Am I recovering? Absolutely. Have I made a lot of progress? I know that I have. Recovered? To say this means that my recovery is finished, and I don't want to make this claim. I haven't crossed any kind of finish line.

Yes, I'm doing well in the symptom check-off aspect of recovery, but my depression is also a power that took control of my life. From my experience, I'd say that the list of symptoms provided by NIMH is accurate and complete. I'd also say that it is just as accurate to describe depression as a fire-breathing dragon gone rogue in your mind. Once you've seen the dragon, you can't be sure it's gone away forever.

I continue in my recovery, accepting it as ongoing, celebrating the progress I have made. The truth is that in the very best and healthiest sense I don't want it to stop. On many days, my life is better than it has ever been, not just better than before I went into the hospital, but literally better than it's ever been. I've learned things in recovery that I never knew, and they have made me happier and my life far more satisfying than it's ever been. Why would I want to stop recovering?

In *The Noonday Demon*, Andrew Solomon writes:

> In good spirits, some love themselves and some love others and some love work and some love God: any of these passions can furnish that vital sense of purpose that is the opposite of depression.[68]

I share all of these passions. They are reflected in my choices to return to work, to be at Vail Place, to tell my story, to fight stigma, and to write this book. They are reflected in my ongoing quest, looking to God and my diagnosis so I can understand what happened to me. Living with such vitality and passion, I think that the worst of depression is over for me. If I'm wrong and the dragon does come back, I will not fight it alone.

Endnotes

1   *Hope for Recovery*, 62.
2   Brown, *I Thought*, 241.
3   *Cool Runnings*, DVD, dir. Turteltaub.
4   Whitman, *Leaves of Grass*, 53.
5   Whitman, *Leaves of Grass*, 154.
6   Burns, *Feeling Good*, 174.
7   Burns, *Feeling Good*, 174.
8   Norris, *Acedia & Me*, 13.
9   *Raising Arizona*, DVD, dir. Coen.
10   Brown, *I Thought*, 93.
11   Brown, *I Thought*, 93.
12   Covington, *Salvation on Sand Mountain*, 3.
13   Burns, *Feeling Good*, 34.
14   Burns, *Feeling Good*, 34.
15   Dickinson, *Poems of Emily Dickinson*, 140.
16   Dickinson, *Poems of Emily Dickinson*, 140.
17   *Breakfast at Tiffany's*, DVD, dir. Edwards.
18   Parker, *Catskill Eagle*, 122.
19   Burns, *Feeling* Good, 40.
20   Burns, *Feeling Good*, 40.
21   Robinson, *Gilead*, 90.
22   Bradshaw, *Healing the Shame*, 237.
23   *Independence Day*, Blu-ray, dir. Emmerich.
24   *Dr. Zhivago*, DVD, dir. Lean.
25   *Twelve Steps*, 125.
26   McGonigal, "Make Stress Your Friend," June 11, 2013.
27   Sher, *Noticer's Guide*, 3.
28   Solomon, *Noonday Demon*, 130.
29   Brueggemann, *Message of the Psalms*, 52.
30   Taylor, *Altar in the World*, 117.
31   Solomon, *Noonday Demon*, 104.
32   Solomon, *Noonday Demon*, 310.
33   Solomon, *Noonday Demon*, 309.
34   Goodwin, *Team of Rivals*, 98–99.

35   Styron, *Darkness Visible*, 58.

36   Art Quotes, "O'Keeffe," Construction category.

37   *Bull Durham*, Blu-ray, dir. Shelton.

38   Norris, *Acedia & Me*, 59.

39   *Bull Durham*, Blu-ray, dir. Shelton.

40   Lovell, "George Saunder's Advice," July 31, 2013.

41   Brody, "Personal Health," September 25, 2001.

42   Brody, "Personal Health," September 25, 2001.

43   Hillerman, *Ghostway*, 43.

44   Didion, *Slouching Towards Bethlehem*, 148.

45   Burns, *Feeling Good*, 38.

46   Solomon, *Noonday Demon*, 103.

47   Norris, *Acedia & Me*, 81.

48   Goodwin, *Team of Rivals*, 99.

49   Golant and Golant, *What to Do*, 82.

50   Neraas, *Apprenticed to Hope*, 38.

51   Palmer, *Let Your Life Speak*, 63.

52   Palmer, *Let Your Life Speak*, 63–64.

53   Brown, *I Thought*, 82.

54   Brown, *I Thought*, 83.

55   Serani, *Living with Depression*, 46.

56   Serani, *Living with Depression*, 46.

57   Krakauer, *Into Thin Air*, 314,

58   Burns, *Feeling Good*, 39.

59   Solomon, *Noonday Demon*, 58.

60   Serani, *Living with Depression*, 10.

61   Taylor, *Altar in the World*, 125.

62   Whitman, *Leaves of Grass*, 53.

63   *Rio Bravo*, DVD, dir. Hawks.

64   Greenstein, "Fight Mental Health Stigma," NAMI (blog), October 11, 2017.

65   Armstrong, *Spiral Staircase*, 175.

66   Stossel, *My Age of Anxiety*, 336.

67   NIMH, "Depression Basics," Section: What are the signs?

68   Solomon, *Noonday Demon*, 15.

Resources

BIBLIOGRAPHY

Armstrong, Karen. *The Spiral Staircase: My Climb Out of Darkness*. New York: Anchor, 2005.

Art Quotes. "Georgia O'Keeffe Quotes." http://www.art-quotes.com/auth_search.php?authid=69.

Boss, Pauline. *Ambiguous Loss: Learning to Live with Unresolved Grief*. Cambridge, MA: Harvard University Press, 1999.

Bradshaw, John. *Healing the Shame That Binds You*. Deerfield Beach, FL: Health Communications, 1988.

Brody, Jane E. "Personal Health; Grieving When the Lost Are Never Found." *New York Times*, September 25, 2001.

Brown, Brené. *The Gifts of Imperfection: Let Go of Who You Think You're Supposed to Be and Embrace Who You Are*. Center City, MN: Hazelden, 2010.

———. *I Thought It Was Just Me (but it isn't): Making the Journey from "What Will People Think?" to "I Am Enough."* New York: Avery, 2008.

Brueggemann, Walter. *The Message of the Psalms: A Theological Commentary*. Minneapolis: Augsburg, 1984.

———. *Praying the Psalms: Engaging Scripture and Life of Faith*. 2nd ed. Eugene, OR: Cascade, 2007.

Burns, David D. *Feeling Good: The New Mood Therapy*. New York: Quill, 2000.

Covington, Dennis, *Salvation on Sand Mountain: Snake Handling and Redemption in Southern Appalachia*. Reading, MA: Addison-Wesley, 1995.

Dickinson, Emily. *The Poems of Emily Dickinson: Reading Edition*. Edited by R. W. Franklin. Cambridge, MA: Belknap, 1999.

Didion, Joan. *Slouching Towards Bethlehem*. New York: Delta, 1969.

Golant, Mitch, and Susan Golant. *What to Do When Someone You Love Is Depressed: A Practical, Compassionate, and Helpful Guide*. 2nd ed. New York: Holt Paperback, 2007.

Goodwin, Doris Kearns. *Team of Rivals: The Political Genius of Abraham Lincoln*. New York: Simon and Schuster Paperbacks, 2006.

Griggs, Robert. *A Pelican of the Wilderness: Depression, Psalms, Ministry, and Movies*. Eugene, OR: Cascade, 2014.

Hillerman, Tony. *The Ghostway*. New York: Avon, 1984.

Hope for Recovery: Participant Manual. Minnesota: National Alliance on Mental Illness, n.d.

Krakauer, Jon. *Into Thin Air: A Personal Account of the Mount Everest Disaster*. New York: Anchor, 1998.

Lovell, Joel. "George Saunders's Advice to Graduates." *New York Times*, July 31, 2013.

McGonigal, Kelly. "How to Make Stress Your Friend." TEDGlobal 2013; September 4, 2013.

National Alliance on Mental Illness. *NAMI Blog*; "9 Ways to Fight Mental Health Stigma," blog entry by Laura Greenstein, October 11, 2017, https://www.nami.org/blogs/nami-blog/october-2017/9-ways-to-fight-mental-health-stigma.

National Institute of Mental Health. "Depression Basics." https://www.nimh.nih.gov/health/publications/depression/index.shtml.

Neraas, Julie. *Apprenticed to Hope: A Sourcebook for Difficult Times*. Minneapolis: Augsburg, 2009.

Norris, Kathleen. *Acedia & Me: A Marriage, Monks, and a Writer's Life*. New York: Riverhead, 2008.

Palmer, Parker. *Let Your Life Speak: Listening for the Voice of Vocation*. San Francisco: Jossey-Bass, 2000.

Parker, Robert. B. *A Catskill Eagle*. New York: Dell, 1985.

Robinson, Marilynne. *Gilead*. New York: Picador, 2004.

Serani, Deborah. *Living with Depression: Why Biology and Biography Matter Along the Path to Hope and Healing*. Lanham, MD: Rowman and Littlefield, 2012.

Sher, Margery Leveen. *The Noticer's Guide to Living and Laughing: Change Your Life Without Changing Your Routine*. The Did Ya Notice? ProjectTM LLC. Privately published, 2014.

Solomon, Andrew. *The Noonday Demon: An Atlas of Depression*. New York: Scribner, 2003.

Stossel, Scott. *My Age of Anxiety: Fear, Hope, Dread, and the Search for Peace of Mind*. New York: Vintage, 2015.

Styron, William. *Darkness Visible: A Memoir of Madness*. New York: Vintage, 1992.

Taylor, Barbara Brown. *An Altar in the World: A Geography of Faith*. New York: HarperOne, 2009.

Twelve Steps and Twelve Traditions. NY: Alcoholics Anonymous World Services, 1965.

Whitman, Walt. *Leaves of Grass: The Original 1855 Edition*. Edited by Laura Ross. NY: Sterling Innovation., 2010.

FILMOGRAPHY

Breakfast at Tiffany's, DVD, directed by Blake Edwards, 1961. Hollywood, CA: Paramount Home Entertainment, 2009.

Bull Durham, Blu-ray, directed by Ron Shelton, 1988. Beverly Hills, CA: Twentieth Century Fox Home Entertainment, 2018.

Cool Runnings, DVD, directed by Jon Turteltaub, 1993. Burbank, CA: Walt Disney Videos, 1999.

Doctor Zhivago: Deluxe Edition, DVD, directed by David Lean, 1965. Burbank, CA: Warner Home Video, 2011.

Independence Day, Blu-ray, directed by Roland Emmerich, 1996. Beverly Hills, CA: Twentieth Century Fox, 2010.

Raising Arizona, DVD, directed by Joel Coen, 1987. Beverly Hills, CA: Twentieth Century Fox Home Entertainment, 2009.

Rio Bravo, DVD, directed by Howard Hawks, 1959. Burbank, CA: Warner Home Video, 2010.

Tootsie, DVD, directed by Sydney Pollack, 1982. Culver City, CA: Sony Pictures Home Entertainment, 2008.

CPSIA information can be obtained
at www.ICGtesting.com
Printed in the USA
JSHW010917051219
2751JS00008B/17

9 781532 683466